THE UGLY HOUSE

THE UGLY HOUSE

FINDING HOME IN GOD'S WORK
OF SALVATION AND SANCTIFICATION

Vanessa Shepherd

This book is dedicated to my grandmother, Norma, who loves the Lord with all of her heart and prays faithfully for her family to know Him and trust Him as she has throughout her life.

Everyone needs a Norma next-door.

Unless otherwise indicated, Scripture quotations are from the ESV® Bible (The Holy Bible, English Standard Version. ESV® Text Edition: 2016. Copyright © 2001 by Crossway Bibles, a publishing ministry of Good News Publishers.)

Scripture quotations marked MSG® are taken from The Message® version of The Holy Bible, copyright © 1993, 2002, 2018 by Eugene H. Peterson

All emphasis on Scripture notations have been added by the author.

Library of Congress Cataloging-in-Publication Data

Library of Congress Control Number: 2024925380

Trade paperback ISBN: 979-8-9920714-1-2
Paperback ISBN: 979-8-9920714-0-5
ePub ISBN: 979-8-9920714-2-9

CONTENTS

Short Story: The Ugly House. 1

Introduction 13

PART ONE: *Salvation*

1. A House Neglected 25

2. Guests and Thefts 37

3. A Hurricane of Hurt 49

4. Who Paid the Price? 61

PART TWO: *Sanctification*

5. A Mailbox Full 75

6. Locks and *the* Key 87

7. The Most Secure System 97

   Psalms to Pray 111

8. Fences for Good Futures 117

9. Good Guard Dogs 129

10. Pictures on the Wall 139

11. Neighbors Next Door 149

   Promises to Hold On to 161

Conclusion 165

Notes 177

THE ^ugly HOUSE

I walked past it every morning on my usual walk; the most grotesque, dilapidated heap of wood that was unabashedly plopped right in the middle of our quaint little neighborhood. I am not even sure that it was livable and by the looks of things it hadn't been for a long time. This was "the ugly house", as the kids would call it, and it was a wonder that it had not been demolished already. Condemned to be sure.

If you were some sort of creative with an eye for the unseen you might imagine that underneath all of that chaos were a few good bones - especially if you are a chronic thrift store treasure hunter with an adrenaline rush for a good project. But friend, this would take more time and energy than you or a small army would have. *But sure, we'll chalk it up to good bones.*

I heard stories of its glory days when it first went up. It had all of the markers for something truly promising. A wrap-around porch that allowed you to get a panoramic view of the countryside. Large, cascading windows to let in the morning sun. The largest kitchen you've ever seen to do all of the baking and entertaining that you could ever want to do. And then - as things do - it fell into some unfortunate hands and after a lot of house parties, a constant rotation of rowdy overnight guests, and a break-in (or two) there wasn't a lot left to be desired. And what was left, well a few natural disasters took care of those.

So this, this is what we are left to look at as we stroll by on our otherwise peaceful morning walks before getting ready for our day. *The ugly house. It almost makes my coffee taste bad. Almost.*

All of this is why it threw me off guard when I first noticed that interest had been taken in the house with the boarded-up windows and Cobb-webbed filled landing. It took me by surprise when the for-sale sign disappeared almost as suddenly as it had been put up.

I guess someone really needed those $5. Or maybe it was a mistake and no one really wanted to take credit for letting it fall into this condition.

I had considered a few other options when the locksmith appeared, replacing all of the locks. *Because burglars can't see the broken windows should they have forgotten to snag some more kindling on their last raid of the place.*

A security system went in next. *Ad nasueum.* It might have almost been comical had it not felt so serious.

Who.
Wants.
This??

What are they actually hoping to catch on camera?

I basically had given up all sense of reason when the fence was being built and the sign for the guard dog was hung.

Finally, I had to ask but I wasn't walking up and knocking on the front door. Their dog seemed nice enough but "Sparky's bite is worse than his bark" gave me some pause and I settled on inquiring of the lovely woman sitting outside of her house next door.

"Can you believe someone actually paid for this place?" I coughed up. "You'd think the owners would have had to pay someone to get out of it".

Of course, I was just being nosey. I had places to be but I didn't want to come right out and say *hey lady that I've walked on the other side of the street to avoid, who bought this dump?*

She smiled that kind of smile that I imagine only comes with age when time starts fading and everything slows down like we have time to chit-chat about the weather or our grandkids. Of course, I had no such time and I think she picked up on that. *My face hides nothing.*

"You'll never believe it, but the Builder bought the house and moved in a while back. I remember when he was building it, you know he built mine, too. Maybe there's hope for it yet."

I could feel a whole conversation coming on that frankly I wasn't emotionally prepared for, so I raised my brows and nodded as if agreeing with her erratic sense of hope. *When pigs fly could the Ugly House ever be worth anything again - I don't care if the president moved in and made it a national monument.*
But, I digress,

Yay for the windows maybe getting replaced and a coat of paint slapped on it so it wouldn't be such a train wreck or drain on everyone else's property. *Insert the biggest eye roll of all time.*

I watched the house more closely now.

I didn't have my neighbor's blind faith that it would be anything of value again, whatever her name was, but it was kind of like watching a dumpster fire. You know it will be messy, maybe smell a little, but it might be fun to watch.

Spring turned to summer and summer to fall. Nothing major to report. Seriously. The dog barks if you get too nosey and try to peek in, not that I have done such a thing, but I guess there are new windows and he swept the porch a bit so there's that. Also, there is a barrage of trucks that pile through. Cleaners and steamers and furniture makers. I wanted to give the Builder a list of all of the outside items that needed attention as well but I had a feeling His hands were full.

The weeks turned to months and all of a sudden - and ever so slowly - those months turned to years. Over time that house wasn't such an eyesore anymore. I can't tell you one specific day that made any difference but maybe it was all of the small things that filled up each day along the way.

And that lovely next-door neighbor, well Norma and I are on friendly terms these days and you'd be shocked to know that I have even had some coffee with her on her porch a time or two.

My coffee was always poured into my travel mug because I wasn't actually going to commit for any longer than absolutely necessary to get the newest updates on what was going on, but still - we're friends.

One day everything lined up perfectly for me to watch the Builder hanging frames on the living room walls. You should have seen the joy on his face when He looked at each of those family portraits. The kind of loving look that you only see in movies when the reality of actual conversations about politics or parenting tactics or cultural ideologies haven't crept into your Thanksgiving dinners.

I was mesmerized by Him.

We rounded the decade mark and honestly, Norma was right. The Builder knew exactly what He was doing. It was incredible. It was the highlight of my walk. Even Sparky let me pet him a time or two and that turned out to be a delight.

I had to thank the Builder for giving our neighborhood back something of worth so I gathered my courage one day and set to knock on the front door.

Gripping the ornate brass door knocker I thought to myself that it was so interesting how it was obviously handcrafted and beautifully unique yet somehow so familiar. Because I have tapped on many a door knockers. That's a lie. No I have not.

But now that I was thinking of it, *I had. Hadn't I?*

As soon as I had come to the end of my thought, the door was opened. It was just the Builder and I staring at each other now.

I had a head full of questions after all of this time but truly the only thing that I could muster up after the longest most awkward pause was,
"Why?"

Not even a complete question and surely something that would need more context to fully understand or even reply to, but the Builder smiled the brightest smile as if elated to see me on the doorstep and finished my thought before I could even think it.

"Because I love this house. I always have. Ever since I first designed it. I hated how it had been turned over and treated over the years so I paid whatever I had to in order to buy it back."

Whatever He had to turned out to be a lot more than $5.

To my shock, it was the most I had ever heard of anyone paying for a house.

I didn't know if He was clinically insane or if He knew something that the rest of us didn't.

His face, His face made me think that it had something to do with the latter which is why I stepped foot into the home the Builder made and remade again. Call it pent-up years of exhausting curiosity... or unequivocal anticipation for something you could only imagine to be the most fulfilling day of your life... but I embraced whatever it was and made my way inside His home.

It took me a moment to take it all in. The craftsmanship and attention to detail were too magnanimous to comprehend in just one glance. I poured over each detail as if inspecting a work of art and drank in all of its beauty as slowly as I possibly could to enjoy it as long as He would allow.

There were still paint buckets and tools and cleaning supplies scattered about as the work was still ongoing, but the living room - the heart of the house - had been perfectly restored as if it had never known the pain of the years before.

My eyes caught the reflection of the light bouncing off of the family portraits He had hung so many years ago, and I stared back at the faces with utter confusion.

The small child in the frame looked just like me. My vision became blurred by the sudden onset of water in my eyes. And then one such element rolled down my cheek. I followed it to the floor where it fell and left my head hanging for some time before I heard His voice again through my own banging thoughts.

"What do you think of the house?" He whispered.

I didn't know how or why but I realized what had been happening all along.

It was *my* home. The Ugly House was me.

His hand reached out as if discerning my unspoken revelation and I lifted my eyes just high enough to see what He was offering to me.

"These are the keys", He said warmly, "They are mine but they are also for you. The ones you've been using are ill-fitting and have caused some damage to the door. But I fixed all of that." Things came into focus now as if I had lived my whole life blind but could now see, "I want you to move back in so we can finish up the rest of the house together".

A wave of emotion came over me and for the first time in a long time, I felt fully alive.

All of these years of seeing but not perceiving, hearing but never knowing, I had become lifeless and cold. Beaten down to the very core of my being by my own choices and those of others, but the Builder saw something in me that I had long forgotten.

Worth.

Value.

Purpose.

All of the things that I had abandoned to live some other life thinking that they could never return to the Ugly House again but through the Builder had all slowly made their way back.

I had given up on that house long ago. But He didn't.
I had spoken the cruelest of words over each part. But He didn't.

I thought the world would be better off without it. But He didn't.

There was still much work to be done and I would have felt too overwhelmed had it not been for His strength and persistence to see it through.

He wasn't going to stop until I was *perfectly* restored. And I have a feeling that it will take my whole life until it's done. But with every cup of coffee that I enjoy with Norma around my kitchen table, in a glass mug these days, and every evening of playing cards or board games with a small group of friends that I had kept at an arm's length for too long, I realize that I'm not in a hurry.

We will get there, the Builder and I.

It will be sure to get messy again as houses do, but I have planted myself firmly within its framework ready with broom in hand. Just as the Builder showed me.

We will finish the work that was started.

And until that day, I'll be eternally grateful for what the Builder did for me all those years back and every day since.

From the locks and the alarm system to the dogs and the fence that protected something so valuable, even when I couldn't see it and especially as we continue the hard work.

Because the Ugly House was me but I don't live there anymore. I'm (*being made*) new.

let this
be your
welcome
home

Introduction

Whether you knew where the story was headed or found yourself surprised at the same revelation our protagonist had found themselves, the truth is that we are all the Ugly House.

I don't mean to offend you or to imagine you as some ogre of a human being. What I mean is that we have all had our own experiences of being pulled through the ringer leaving us a bit on the side of "damaged goods". For many, you have found the hope that we will talk about in these pages but you have yet to wrestle with the darkness of your suffering or accept the call to live in a transformed way. Both are necessary, both require hard work and dedication. And both offer exponential dividends to the quality of life that God has laid out before us.

And for the rest, the ones who picked this book out by sheer happenstance or out of insistent recommendation by a friend, if you have not yet met the Builder it would be my great honor to introduce you. Of course, the beginning story is just that, a story, but the implications and the genuine feelings for you are true.

We are forever the passer-by; prone to distraction, discontentment, and disconnection. And God, forever the Builder draws us home.

Something I am just too ordinary to communicate to its fullest - but something I will do my best to convey with what I have been given in our time together. Me with the words and you with the sharing of your time to hear them.

To start us off I will share that this was a daydream that I have held in my heart for over a decade now. The house, the hurting, and all of the ways God steps in to help. I thought it was meant for a specific moment in time.

A girl's only talk at a youth camp no less.

I was asked to be the main speaker for this specific service and it was quite an honor. I too had attended this same youth camp as a teenager and it was humbling to be the one in the front of the room.

Clutching the handful of notes that I had typed out about the house that I saw in my head, I started things off with everyone's eyes closed, imagining their dream home.

Full disclosure, I was not the girl to dream about my wedding while at the kindergarten table. You might have had better luck finding me near the outdoor chalkboard writing a story or inside the playhouse teaching an unfortunate soul my version of "school". So when asked to bring something to mind of such grandeur and beauty, I knew that some may have an image right away and others could have been frustrated by that suggestion altogether.

Who knows themselves perfectly enough to definitively state that they could design an entire house to live in happily forever... at the age of fifteen?

I could barely decide what I wanted to wear each day.

For some reason that simple task had become a chore.

Still, I asked.

I might not have had the full picture myself, but the wrap-around porch - I knew that had to be in mine. And slowly I could see the girls smile as they imagined more and more of their perfectly built and beautifully stylized refuge that they were piecing together up in their heads.

Of course, those ideas of idealism crumbled when I then had the audacity to ask that each girl see *themselves* as that uniquely crafted and wholly intentional structure.

How dare I?

Scripture is actually the first to illustrate us as a "temple" so it wasn't even a completely unique idea to liken us in this way. And while there may be a time or two of head nodding to "Brick House" by the Commodores, no person actually wants to be described as one.

It isn't just the idea of being called a whole structure that brings offense, it is also the image of something in a perfected desirable state that is frustrating to us.

There is always a more evident list of things "wrong" with us than ever a picture of things designed on purpose and perfectly right. I have toe-thumbs. There, I said it. The actual term for it is "Brachydactyly type D" and has also been known to be referred to as "murderer's thumbs", so yeah. Fifteen-year-old Vanessa was not imagining my murdering toe thumbs to be something dreams are made of.

My ears also stick out far beyond culturally acceptable. I only knew to hate them as soon as it became apparent that they would be the cause of my incessant teasing by boys who I now know were just insecure themselves. Rationally the only thing to do was to keep my hair down (pre-knowing how to actually straighten or curl it) or to pull it back in a low George-Washington ponytail so they could remain hidden.

That should go to prove my deep understanding of the disdain I was received with as I myself was better emotionally prepared to be considered a founding father than to be noticed for having ears.

With all of the issues of self-esteem and suffering of the teenage years, I boxed up that message and put it away when our time was done with. It was surely for this time, in this place. My ideas of living a life honoring to God as a young woman against the otherwise love-less and identity-less challenges of purity culture (the popularized method for teaching teenage girls about modesty and sexual abstinence through shame and fear) had prayerfully made their mark and I was happy to have come and gone the same.

If anyone needed to hear the message of value it was a room full of teenagers. Surely as I aged I would find that the rest of the world had already figured out what hormones and improper hygiene were hiding.

But that house, that broken down and brutalized shell of a home, stuck with me for all these years. I kept on seeing it. Everywhere.

Chalk it up to Sentimentalism for the whole full-circle experience, or Emotionalism for now having a daughter of my own, but the truth is that I cannot stray too far from the message of it being one for us all.

We are the Ugly House.

Undervalued. Abused. Neglected.

And my commitment to you is that I will spend every word on every page to persuade you to believe in the dream of that house again.

Because **we never take care of what we don't care for.**

This isn't a self-help book. Although I do believe firmly in the truth that honoring God's design for our lives does in fact help us.

This is a plea for the value of humanity book. A war against the fixation on behavior modification book. A drawing back to the fondness you once found in faith book. A challenge to the cultural war on interdependent community book, so we can love our neighbors *as we love ourselves* (Mark 12:31). I might not call it all of those things elsewhere - it is quite a mouthful - but if you are to know what you are getting into then let me simplify it to just this: The Ugly House is a love letter from a dear friend to come home.

Don't push it away.
Don't call it too mushy for your brazen personality.

I can deflect with the best of them. I will do my best to share some of my story here on these pages and be honest with my experiences and attitudes. Not because I have reached some level of spiritual perfection, but because **you can't build a house with fake bricks.**

No one benefits from pretending.

And if we cannot first receive love then we are doomed to ever be able to truly give it.

This is your chance to dip out. To keep on pretending that the way you are living could never benefit from an honest look in the mirror. Just as the Ugly House portrayed, and I really should give that main character a name for all of our sakes, we are forced to face our true selves every day. If we recognize it or not.

A glance in the mirror as you brush your teeth each morning, a moment of reflection after losing your mind over a small annoyance, or a forced quiet drive with just you and your thoughts as your iPhone stops connecting to the Bluetooth stereo on your way to work.

Your humanity is never permanently covered no matter how deep you try to bury it.

Look away or lean in, the choice is up to you.

But my friend, I pray you choose to stay. Because what God desires to create is far beyond your wildest dreams. If you dare to look and truly see it.

This isn't about brick and mortar, it's about you, and God's work of putting you back together again. The way He dreamed you up in the first place. **You were always**

intended as a masterpiece. This story is about getting a peak at the real you.

But the you that hasn't yet existed. The *future* you.

> "Imagine yourself as a living house. God comes in to rebuild that house. At first, perhaps, you can understand what He is doing. He is getting the drains right and stopping the leaks in the roof and so on; you knew that those jobs needed doing and so you are not surprised. But presently He starts knocking the house about in a way that hurts abominably and does not seem to make any sense. What on earth is He up to? The explanation is that He is building quite a different house from the one you thought of - throwing out a new wing here, putting on an extra floor there, running up towers, making courtyards. You thought you were being made into a decent little cottage: but He is building a palace. He intends to come and live in it Himself." (CS Lewis, "Mere Christianity")[1]

What would a house like this take? What kind of work should we prepare ourselves for? What kind of things should we put in place to protect the work being done from future harm that may come?

That is what I hope that we are able to unpack - the full spectrum of inner work and outer guards that are all a part of the process of growing into the palace that God is designing. I don't want it to seem overwhelming or impossible - none of this life is about perfection. Something I like to tell my own brain often as I am a chronic obsessor of doing things perfectly. The point is intentionality, not letting the work that is being done be forgotten or left vulnerable. It isn't giant leaps but baby steps in the right direction with eyes wide open that are going to make the most difference.

As Anna from Frozen 2 sang, it's choosing "the next right thing". Yes, I did quote that, you're welcome. I hope you sang it for full effect. She was onto something.

It isn't about comparing how far you are from the big picture but focusing on the next step toward that end goal. That's how we get there. That's how we persevere. That's how God makes us into the building of His creation and our dreams.

This is how.

personal reflection

1. What would your life as a house look like? On the next page, take a moment to sketch, make a list, or write a poem about how you see yourself right now.

PART ONE

salvation

CHAPTER ONE

A House Neglected

Tugging at my sleeves to hide my hands as if wanting to claw my way inside of the sweater I was wearing to escape the moment, the pastor continued his long drawn-out message about... something. Truthfully, I barely remember anything he had said. Not because it was just another Sunday morning at church and the memories all faded together. No, this time it was just him and I in his office after my frantic mother had found that I had cut myself again and on the way to the Psychiatric Hospital she claimed to be driving me to, she stopped by the church instead.

I might have preferred the quiet respite of a solitary hospital room in that moment, but still, I made no attempts to leave. I wasn't fighting, wasn't running, I had simply already left my own self as I had been in the habit of doing to manage real life. They have a term for it now, maybe they did then too, but as I have grown older I have learned a lot about the survival mechanism of disassociation. It is my constant temptation when going through hardship and therefore something I vowed to learn. A bit of a "know your enemy" tactic.

As I sat in the leather studded chair of that stuffy office surrounded by books about the gospel, I was realizing that the very action of cutting to deal with my inner pain was more of a problem for others than I had ever given it credit. I didn't understand and wanted to ask why it was such a big deal. I believed I had done the honorable thing of saving others the heartache of having to deal with me. And I wasn't cutting so deep that I was putting myself in danger. It was just my way of remembering that I was alive. Like despite the trauma, somewhere deep down there still existed a girl who knew that things were wrong, and things should be felt, but that the world was unsafe. So I exited stage left.

I had become an observer of my own life and when things would pile up I would search to feel something, anything, again. Even if it was just the small sting of a blade against my wrist or hips. A visual representation of my emotional suffering just to know I was still somewhere in there.

I said that I *barely* remembered anything because it wasn't all a waste, there was something from that afternoon in his office that I do remember.

It was how he spoke to me. Gentle, not full of condemnation. And genuine, not repulsed by what I now realize is a hard-to-stomach self-destructive coping habit for others to witness.

He said in a roundabout way, "If we don't face the things that are hurting us and we just shove it all inside, it is like a dresser drawer. Someday it won't close anymore. Someday everything will just come pouring out."

There is this song that remarks how "it's a slow fade when you give yourself away" and I have known that and seen that to be true. The choice to distance ourselves from the person we are or have become is never an overnight decision. It is a series of failures or critiques. It's a harsh word spoken when we needed more grace and an even colder welcome when we needed a safe place to retreat.

It is the abuse and abandonment and isolation of our pasts coupled with the frustrations and sufferings of our present.

That house wasn't emptied from the soul inside without cause.

There is confusion and hardship and survival mechanisms that make feeling into an impossible task. It helped you for a season. You journeyed a hard road and made it, that's for sure.

But now what?

You left the house and it has become a stranger to you. How do you imagine moving back inside?

Here's the harder question - do you want to? Because what if you don't? What if you don't like that house and have lost hope for it to become anything of value to anyone again?

How can we even go on talking about ways to find healing and growth when you are staring at the front door unsure if you even want to return?

How does someone who out of necessity protected themselves from feeling the difficulties of life now suddenly come to the decision that they are ready to embrace the full spectrum of human experiences?
Because not feeling is way easier than feeling, and to understand the Ugly House we have to first recognize that

someone had to move out - had to give up - in order for it to have fallen so far.

By choice and by force. It is both.

Let's start here, on the pavement. Deciding if we want to go back in. If we want to face the true condition of our hearts.

It was Jeremiah with the wisdom from God who penned that the "hearts are deceitfully wicked, who could know it". (Jeremiah 17:9) What if it is worse than we imagined? Worse than when we left?

It probably is, friend.

It probably is.

I was twelve years old when I started dreaming of my own death, my own escape. Before then there were small moments of wishful thinking of circumstances that might change, but the girl who left 8th grade is not the same girl who entered 9th.

I hated myself. Would rather be anyone but myself.

And honestly, I truly believed no one even noticed as I slowly drifted into the nothingness of emotionally vacating my own life.

Like a person watching over their body going through the motions of conversations and schoolwork, this is the shell of the girl I had become and life was easier this way.

I couldn't feel the pain anymore. I couldn't feel real joy either, but it was worth the sacrifice.

If someone had taken a few more moments to look into my eyes they might have realized that Elvis had left the building. That I was pretending the best I could to live when in fact I felt like my true self had died.

Was it really a problem? No one seemed to protest as I still accomplished all of my tasks and kept up on all of my responsibilities.

Was this living?

Was this it?

Let's not pretend that we don't share these same thoughts throughout our lifetimes. The idea of living a fuller more fulfilling life than we are *now* is a pretty constant temptation for most.

And then there are the times we just leave. Willingly.

The times we deliberately walk out the front door to discover something that we believe ourselves to be missing. The times we are the leavers and abusers of our own lives, self-destructing to punish or abandoning to forget. Maybe we haven't gotten that far, maybe we're stuck somewhere between being the tempted and confused.

All I know is that sometimes all we need to see is something glimmer when we're already on the edge, to chase it.

My father has actually been known to pull over on the side of busy freeways if he passed a Home Depot bucket on the side of the road. I guess this was a more common occurrence in the Valley of California than I have ever come to know as an adult but the fact that a grown man with the means of buying such a bucket would find not just joy in a plastic utility tool but so much that he would halt his plans and put his life in danger makes it that much more enjoyable to remember.

So really, it doesn't even have to glimmer to be desirable to us. To cause us to set out on our own grand adventure throwing caution to the wind, and ourselves on the alter of something other than what we have.

Robert Robinson summed it up so beautifully when he wrote,
"O to grace how great a debtor
daily I'm constrained to be!
Let that grace now, like a fetter,
bind my wandering heart to thee.
Prone to wander, Lord, I feel it,
prone to leave the God I love;
here's my heart; O take and seal it;
seal it for thy courts above.[2]

We *like* to leave.

The only thing we can truly impose control over is ourselves so let's start with us. Did you feel you had to leave, or did you want to?

And if you wanted to, why?

Temptations are only tempting if we actually desire them, so what was the promise? What did that situation or person hold out in front of you like a carrot in front of a donkey? Was it worth it? I imagine you've come to realize as I did that it was not. Maybe you aren't there yet, but come back when the greener grass isn't green anymore.

These questions aren't meant to interrogate you, they are meant to help us look inward. To examine where our feet are. To see if we can still be found somewhere inside or if we got off the train long ago. So this then becomes my plea, get back on.

We cannot speak for the person last year or even last week, but the one who peers into these pages that is the person with the power to change. To choose again. Choose differently.

Even now I am not sure if I love the person I've become, like I've slipped off the path somewhere and have grown to be a more irritable version of my former self. The truth is that I could have always been this way but maybe I am just now knowing it. With the husband and the kids and the church all tugging at my attention and time, I somehow reverted to a more cynical person than I would ever want to be.

In any case, whether a small leaving or a big one, we can choose to jump back into the hard work. Or tiptoe. Maybe we just tiptoe back.

So take a big breath and ask yourself this, who's in charge here?

It's not your parents or your friends or your boss. Not your significant other or a neighbor or a well-meaning pastor. Do you want to know who actually has the power to move your feet forward? You do. If you want to. If you feel you are worth enough to make the investment into your own heart and life. If you see what God sees, a sinner saved by grace whose been given an incredible opportunity to partner with Him in the work of building.

You are the building. *You are the house.* It's time to move back in. Not to "Ugly" - you were never meant to reside there - no, you were the Dream of the Builder. Move back to the Dream House and begin again. Come *home*.

"For we are God's fellow workers. You are God's field, God's building. According to the grace of God given to me, like a skilled master builder I laid a foundation, and someone else is building upon it. Let each one take care how he builds upon it." (1 Corinthians 3:9-10)

Full context so we are not mistaken, this passage is referring to the whole body of Christ being a field, a building, fit together and meant to be built on by the working of many hands. My intention in using these verses is not to say that it proves exactly my point. The goal is to see how God refers to you, yes YOU, as a "fellow worker" with Him. To show that we are all intended to put our hands to the job in front of us and build. This is the key. Not that we are to be only concerned with our own lives, but that we would partner with God in doing the hard work that often (if not every time) *starts* with our own lives and in our own hearts and continues surrounded by the community that He is fitting together.

We can't build with fake bricks.

And if we aren't committed to the process of being fully present for God to be at work in our lives, then all of the work we could ever do for Him is in vain. None of it will ever be good enough because it is inauthentic from the start.

Start with real, start with you. Where is your heart? Let's start there.

It isn't that we can't work in greater capacities for the Lord, serving in church or our community, until we are perfect. *Bologna*. We never will be. That's a lie told to you to keep the Lord from moving in and through you as He's gifted. Serve. Make a mistake and repent. Serve again.

But we at the very least have to be present in our own bodies (mentally, physically, emotionally, and spiritually) in the process.

That is how the real work gets done. That is how we become the real building that His Spirit dwells in.

"Do you not know that you [this is plural, like "you all"] are God's temple and that God's Spirit dwells in you? If anyone destroys God's temple, God will destroy him. For God's temple is holy, and you are that temple."
1 Corinthians 3:16-17

So if you are on the outside of that house, *your house*, and wondering if it's time to head back inside - the answer is yes.

No matter what you face when you get inside, the Builder is there too. He never leaves us to manage on our own. (Because we couldn't. Honestly, this life can be terrible and I have no idea how people can do it without the Lord.)

Knock on the door, step over the threshold, behold the face of your Creator. He's been waiting for you to come back to yourself.

Your new life starts today.

personal reflection

1. In what areas have you given up hope that God could/ would restore you?

2. What is your current response to stress? (Fight, flight, and freeze are widely used terms. An additional fourth response called "fawning" has been newly identified for those who are prone to please their way out of a situation.)

3. Are there any areas that you have run from or walked out of that God is bringing to attention for you to journey through with Him?

CHAPTER TWO

Guests and Thefts

There's not much like the mad dash to "clean the house" when someone has been invited over. It is a much different process than the normal every day tidying up. Somehow, the standard starts to include places a guest would never venture but has suddenly become of utmost importance.

When you are an adult with some strong leanings toward OCD this of course means nothing. Every day I clean in places where guests will not be visiting. But one of my favorite comments ever made by my child when cleaning up for a guest was after I asked him to really tidy up his room.

His confused and matter-of-fact response was simply, "why? Will they be eating in there?"

He wasn't wrong. I laughed of course. And then asked him to carry on tidying up anyway. Because sometimes it isn't lost on me that it does sound a tad insane.

We take a lot of effort to prepare our homes for friends and family to visit - but do you know what takes more work? Cleaning up after them.

Sure there are some who offer to help with the dishes or by putting their chair back to the place it came from if more had to be brought out, but more times than not there was a bit of dirt dragged in where the floor had been just swept, crumbs on the table that had been perfectly set for dinner, and pillows in a random order that they certainly don't go in.

Not to mention, the trashes are more full, the bathroom towels a bit more used, and if they've brought children with them... a whole room of toys to clean up. You'd be lucky if it is just one room.

Having people come over is the absolute best and sometimes absolutely exhausting.

Especially for birthdays or celebrations that include dozens of people all under one roof.

I imagine the Ugly House had many such parties in it's hey-day. Because who doesn't want to share the joy of friendship in personal spaces? (*Unless of course you aren't a fan of that space... and then you become the traveler or the hermit. If it has been awhile since you have invited anyone in, start with seeing value in the house again like we talked about in Chapter 1.*)

Community is a gift from God. All throughout scripture we are not just encouraged but shown how the people of God live amongst each other in neediness of one another. I don't love that word "needy" either, but let's reframe it to be more of a connection to one another (like a body part that works correctly in conjunction with other body parts) and not a codependency as if our very well-being depends on someone else.

Paul even encourages the church in Rome in this way toward greater community and hospitality when he penned:

"For as in one body we have many members, and the members do not all have the same function, so we, though many, are one body in Christ, and individually members one of another. Having gifts that differ according to the grace given to us, let us use them... Let love be genuine. Abhor what is evil; hold fast to what is good. Love one another with brotherly affection. Outdo one another in showing honor. Do not be slothful in zeal, be fervent in spirit, serve the Lord. Rejoice in hope, be patient in tribulation, be constant in prayer. Contribute to the needs of the saints and seek to show hospitality. Bless those who persecute you; bless and do not curse them. Rejoice with those who rejoice, weep with those who weep." (Romans 12:4-6, 9-15)

The joy of being a friend is that you are there to celebrate, maybe even to weep it says... but not to clean. Nowhere on the list is the mention of taking over the responsibility of cleaning up for someone else. The messes made within our walls are our responsibility to look after. No one, no matter how willing, can de-clutter our hearts or clean up our minds for us.

So when everyone gets into their cars for the night to head home for a full night of sleep, you put your hands into the sink to start on the dishes that are left behind. (Or you wait until the next morning or put everything into the trash because you bought paper plates so you wouldn't have a bigger mess to clean, no judgement from the OCD girl, here.)

Cleaning up our homes is our job. And even the most well-meaning people will leave a mess behind. This is the nature of humanity, that we exist and take up space. Nothing is left the same when we enter another's life.

People take effort. But that effort is worth more than we could ever imagine. Because all of the way back in the beginning of time a God who Himself is always in relationship as the Trinity - three-in-one - saw Adam and declared that in His perfect creation, it was "not good that the man should be alone" (Genesis 2:18).

We need Him AND we need others.

Life isn't good any other way. But life gets messy when we are in community because **people are messy**.

When is the last time that you were in a perfectly normal conversation and a remark was made that was borderline offensive? Or how about the last time you made a comment that seemed perfectly understandable but somehow your intention was misunderstood?

Friends and family take constant care. T**he tangible mess is just a representation of the emotional, mental, and spiritual crumbs that are left for us to be dealt with.** We can ignore it all, sure, but there will be a moment that everything will pile up into an overwhelming heap and suddenly it feels easier to walk away than to start addressing it.

My mother was known to take a rake to my shared-bedroom a time or two growing up. Why a rake, you might ask? Because it is a great tool for reaching far under beds or into the back spaces of a closet where things that had been "tidied up" had started to smell.

My sister and I would stand in front of the biggest pile of literal junk that had been accumulating for who knows how long and wonder why we couldn't just burn it all down to start over.

Actually, my sister would "use the restroom" for an hour or so and then reminisce on every piece of found "treasure" that had seemingly been lost in the abyss but was now found... I however was known to take a trash bag and throw everything away without even looking. Like $10, I threw that away during one such cleaning session because going through the pile to determine what was needed and what was not was not going to happen.

Both responses are so indicative to our behaviors in friendship. A running away from the reality of the hard stuff so we can just hold on to the beautiful parts, or the temptation to trash it all and start over.

I've come to find out, that the constant attention and work of rejoicing and weeping is the most fulfilling way to foster relationships with one another.

The scriptures talk about the grittiness of dealing with the mess (sin) of others and ourselves, and how partaking in the work of repentance and forgiveness can actually heal us: "Therefore, confess your sins to one another and pray for one another, that you may be healed." (James 5:16)

Digging even further into our relationships with others we find this note:
"Brothers, if anyone is caught in any transgression, you who are spiritual should restore him in a spirit of gentleness. Keep watch on yourself, lest you too be tempted. Bear one another's burdens, and so fulfill the law of Christ." (Galatians 6:1-2)

Bearing another person's burdens is not bearing their to-do list, their suffering, or their responsibilities. The word "burden" translates better to "sin", meaning that in a relationship, we quite literally bear each other's sins. Because people are messy. We are messy. And we can't help but spread that mess everywhere we go.

God's idea of friendship is to deal with the mess in love, in prayer, in forgiveness, and with accountability. Friendships help us stay on the narrow path, growing more and more into the image of God. They help us to become the best versions of ourselves that God designed when He formed us. To put it simply, all relationships (with God and others) are for our sanctification. "Iron sharpens iron, and one man sharpens another." (Proverbs 27:17)

One of the best ways the enemy of your soul can think of keeping you stuck is by cutting you off from life-giving relationships with real offenses and hurtful sins. Then you will have to choose, will you be the conflict avoider or relationship leaver? Pretending that the heaping pile disappears once it is out of sight and out of mind. Or, in a fight against the buildup of an even greater mess inside the home that you are learning to value and cherish, will you choose instead to sit with the aftermath and do the hard and holy work of cleaning up?

That all sounds great of course, but how do you do that?

I once heard Jackie Hill Perry claim that "the church hurt me and the church healed me". If there is a friendship that you've invested your life into, then contending for a genuine and trusted future together will mean inviting them back over to address what had been left behind. They will have some things in the pile to take responsibility for. They will need to know that the pile even exists - because they may not.

Jesus instructs us to focus on the log in our own eyes before pointing out the speck in someone else's because we are terrible at seeing the reality of our own sin (see Matthew 7:3). Who is seeing the world clearly with a tree not just in their purview but nestled in their cornea?

Can we humble ourselves enough to say that we might not be seeing the forest for the trees? The buildup might just be a mutual battering that two people need to give attention to, take responsibility for, repent of, and forgive.

Or it could be a crumb. Something to mention that was left after the wake of an interaction unintentionally, but none-the-less messy and needing of attention. **The more we care for the crumbs the less we are left with a mess.**

Let's make a habit of talking about the small stuff (and making sure to treat it as the small stuff). Because our friendships are of infinite worth, intentionally created to bring goodness to our lives and flourish our souls but their joy is getting snuffed out with the small stuff. Let's catch those little critters that threaten the beauty that is growing. "Catch the foxes for us, the *little* foxes that spoil the vineyards, for our vineyards are in blossom." (Song of Solomon 2:15)

Sneaky foxes.
We may not deal with foxes in our day to day lives. But critters... I am up to my eyeballs in little critters. And I am not talking about the chosen animals that share my home.

Ground hogs. Moles. Raccoons. God bless those raccoons.

The uninvited critters are making even my domesticated pets lose their minds.

One night we had had enough of the little band of raccoons getting into the outdoor storage where we kept our dog food so we placed a very humane, non-lethal, trap and waited in the darkness to see if our plan would work to rid us of their constant nuisance.

Bringing out my phone to capture our triumphant victory, I soon realized that we were in way over our heads as dozens... DOZENS... of raccoons descended onto our back porch to partake in the food placed inside the small cage. They came from the trees, they came from the creek, they came from the ivy growing over our fence.

Never in my life would I have imagined that the little muddy footprints left for us like a kindergarten teacher making leprechaun prints on the desks to delight the children would in fact be a whole army of aggressive vermin.
Sometimes we choose the mess (looking at you, dog, trying to unearth the moles in our yard), and sometimes we are overrun with Satan-sent Mal-intentioned thieves.

A friend is someone who is willing to sit with you to sift through the pile that they take responsibility for contributing to, but a thief is someone who will break into your life with no intention or care for the mess that is left.
The raccoons are not helping me scrub the white patio cushions that I insisted on buying. The dog isn't helping either but at least she's cute.

You know who also isn't helping clean up? The abusive father who learned his ways from an even more abusive father. The brother who is knee-deep in addiction, who can't even crawl out of the prison of his own making. The friend who is so overtaken by grief that her callous words and increased emotional distance make you want to write the whole friendship off. Or the countless acquaintances that are so lost in their own troubles that they cannot see you drowning.

They aren't thieves. They are just helpless to help.

Find the helpers.

The old lady in your church who prays like she is warring in an unseen battle. The therapist with one hand gripping a Bible and the other a whole slew of tools to help you wade through your darkness. The pastor who shows up when everyone else is running out. The friend who comes to grab the kids when you have locked yourself in the closet as you contemplate the deep temptation to abandon your life. The spouse who can't find the right words to say but is committed to standing by you "til death do we part".

All of our helpers will be imperfect, because people are imperfect, but the community that God is placing us into is one that makes messes and helps clean them up. It hurts *and* heals.

When we determine that we are of value and worth (chapter 1) and welcome the mess that means sharing our lives with others, we are one step closer to living the life that God had in mind from the beginning of time.

As the old saying goes, "Don't mind the mess. The kids are making memories."

personal reflection

1. If you were to make note of those closest to you that fall under the Guest category (chosen relationships), are there any residual tensions that need to be addressed?

2. Thieves are those who have done intentional damage to our lives through abusive actions, second-hand harm, or general fallout. How might God be doing a work of healing in these areas?

3. How has forgiveness toward self and others transformed your joy?

CHAPTER THREE

A Hurricane of Hurt

Natural Disasters. We let those words slip off the end of our tongues as if they were just another part of an everyday news cycle, but when you've lived through a natural disaster those two words take on a life of their own.

My husband's twin brother and his father were some of the many who devoted their lives to helping clean up after Hurricane Katrina in the late summer of 2005. This devastating tropical cyclone took the lives of 1,392 people and caused an estimated 186.3 billion dollars worth of damage. The costliest of all storms in history. I remember watching the journalists reporting day after day, horrified that such a thing could happen without cause and for many, without warning.

No one could have known the extent of the destruction.

At its peak, this Category 5 Hurricane hurled winds of 175 mph and caused flooding so severe that 80% of New Orleans remained flooded for weeks afterward.

The hurricane lasted 9 days - but you can still feel the rumblings of its effects all these years later. Why? Because life is not lived as a series of one-time experiences that fade into the distance each night as we lay our heads down to sleep. They continue on. In our memories, in our muscle memory, down to our cellular DNA.

Everything we experience forms us.

Formation is a continual process that if we are not paying attention, can derail much of our progress... and our sleep. We wake up wondering how we got to be so sick, so exhausted, so depressed without realizing that our bodies are holding onto the traumas we've endured.

At this moment in time, it has been 6 years since my brother tragically passed away from injuries sustained in a motorcycle accident one week prior. He was 27 years old. The week after his passing, while planning for his funeral, a great friend and mentor of mine received some incredibly bad news that caused him to take his own life. Both of these losses happened just 18 months after my brother-in-law, who had been fighting an addiction for many years, overdosed in the middle of the night.

These deaths, these horrific disasters, have ripped the roof off of my soul in more ways than I could ever recount. They've exposed the most vulnerable, most stripped-down, version of myself to all who would be close enough to notice.

It is hard to not feel like less of a human after tragedy comes knocking at your door. Not just in the moment. Not just for a short time after. But even now, some days I wake up and sense that I have one foot on earth while the other longs to step into Heaven.

This world holds so much devastation that the afterlife becomes the furthest thing from a threat, or something to keep us on the straight and narrow, it can be a sweet promise that is too good to not want a little early. Something we long for and desire. Like eating your dessert first.

Even Paul himself in prison wrote to those in Philippi: "*Yes, and I will rejoice, for I know that through your prayers and the help of the Spirit of Jesus Christ this will turn out for my deliverance, as it is my eager expectation and hope that I will not be at all ashamed, but that with full courage now as always Christ will be honored in my body, whether by life or by death. For to me to live is Christ, and* **to die is gain**. *If I am to live in the flesh, that means fruitful labor for me. Yet which I shall choose I cannot tell. I am hard pressed between the two.* **My desire is to depart and be with Christ, for that is far better.**" (Phillippians 1:18-23)

Heaven is not a lesser version of this life that we should dread and lose sleep over. That part I knew well. It wasn't the convincing I needed. No, the onslaught of suffering had caused me to lose something that I had not seen coming - the desire to continue living. Not to intentionally cut my time short, but to withdraw and vacate the whole earthly experience.
I could be a shell of a human and none would be the wiser.

That is what I imagined. And it sounded almost spiritual. Like I was having an out-of-body experience, living as I was already part of the heavenly kingdom of God. Was this what the Scriptures intended with our being in this world but not of it?

Turns out, no. And hey, that was not really a surprise.

Because disassociating turned out to be a lesser experience than I had imagined and I didn't have the right building plans to get back on track.

I had come to know what Jesus spoke so plainly of with His disciples, that "in this world you will have trouble." (John 16:33) Truth be told, it didn't take me this long to figure that part out. I could have told you in kindergarten when my teacher forced me to eat something that I didn't like and upon regurgitating it back onto the lunchroom table, then made me clean it up, that this world would be a little troublesome.

This world had some difficulties. That teacher had a lot of them.

Through living, we learn that pain is part of the process. When we take it all of the way back to the Garden of Eden, we see that sin entered and broke everything. Not just the relationship with God that Jesus would come to restore, but the very fabric of His creation. Everything was now tainted. Everything would be touched by sin, and because "the wages of sin is death" (Romans 6:23) then that meant that every part of the world would experience a decay that it had not yet known before.

Trouble. Sin. Death. All of these were just making my list of why it would be better to go through the motions of life with being as mentally and emotionally present-less as possible, but none of that is the abundant life that God promised to us here.

So if I was going to allow myself to feel all of the feelings and experience all of the highs and lows of this world, I wanted God to teach me the secret of the better life that He promised.

Turns out, those same verses that spoke of trouble and death were the same ones with the key to the life that I was looking for.

John 16:33 in its fullness says, "I have told you these things" - which things? Jesus was talking to His disciples about being the Son of God. He was proclaiming His divinity that gave all of His words not just validity but authority! He says "I have told you these things so that in me you may have peace. In this world you will have trouble. But take heart! I have overcome the world."

Romans 6:23 even continues to say, "For the wages of sin is death, but the gift of God is eternal life in Christ Jesus our Lord."

And now for one of my favorites, this verse is so important to our family that my father actually tattooed it onto his arm after my brother had passed:
"Praise be to the God and Father of our Lord Jesus Christ, the Father of compassion and the God of all comfort, who comforts us in all our troubles, so that we can comfort those in any trouble with the comfort we ourselves receive from God. For just as we share abundantly in the sufferings of Christ, so also our comfort abounds through Christ." (2 Corinthians 1:3-5)

The thing that we have all come to know, the thing that the South has always known, is that the storms are inevitable. They are coming. It is not a matter of "if", but "when".

The problem is not that suffering exists, but with living as if it didn't.

That hurricane that devastated the world but especially the South that was forever marred with its destruction, cost more than it ever should have.

More lives.
More destruction.
More costs to repair.

Not because of the storm. The South has always had severe weather patterns. They have learned to accept the sirens and the shelters as part of their lives. The storm wasn't the foe that day, it was the faulty preparations of the levees.

The majority of deaths happened not because of being in the direct path of Hurricane Katrina, but due to the incapable structures that were meant to prevent flooding as most drowned in the deep unescapable waters.

It was the aftermath that took the most lives.

Just as Rome wasn't built in a day, your feelings of overwhelm and anxiety were not capsized with one stressful incident. This was not a one-way street straight from hardship to annihilation.

You have endured many things.
Things you may not even realize or be able to put into words that you've endured.

And just like the Ugly House, you lose a little more of yourself each time. Something gets broken and where there was once a drive to give attention to the broken pieces, there might now exist an acceptance and apathy toward ever being perfectly whole again.

It wasn't that my brother's death took my will to live, it was that it was the *final* straw - the last bit of strength that I had - and I didn't have anymore.

We have been silently enduring the cycle of trauma and aftermath for years of parenting a child with behavioral special needs. What once was an active life of ministry alongside my husband, had devolved after the birth of our son into a permanent response of staying home so as not to upset or alter the usual patterns of our life while sending my husband off to represent us both.

There were days with hours of screaming with no end. I tried all of the tools that I had to comfort and help but could never find the proper way to help him and make it stop. No amount of prayer, restrictions, gentle parenting, discipline, therapy, or classes could provide the relief that my mind and body so desperately needed.

And what's worse - people would either want to blame him for "choosing" to act this way, or blame me for "parenting him to behave like this". I have long understood that I have perfectionistic OCD tendencies and not being able to parent "right", to have a socially acceptable family, as *a pastor*, ate away at my very identity as a mother.

Did I not have enough faith? Was I doing something wrong? Was I being punished?

My child wasn't doing this *to* me, my child needed strength *from* me to be able to have the stability that his brain could not grasp.

But I didn't have much strength left to give.

Years I had battled with walking on eggshells every day, never knowing if he would "grow out of it" as many would say or if it would divulge into something more severe that had riddled my own family of origin. I held my breath for so long that a recent trip to the doctor resulted in being told that I literally needed to "learn how to breathe". I wish I was kidding. Who writes that down on paper?

Friends became sparse, childcare dwindled to none, and my days were full of "rinse and repeat".

His diagnosis didn't get him the empathy that others would receive and those who would understand had children equally dysfunctional making meetups a completely unrealistic dream.

And then after years of emotional and mental struggle, grappling with the mounting body pain that had become my everyday companion due to stress, I picked up the phone one spring day to my sister on the other end sharing that my brother had been in an accident. He was awake and talking but completely paralyzed from the chest down.

I jumped into my parent's car, drove the 5 hours to see him, and spent every waking moment that I possibly could at the hospital, only to have my little brother pass away one week later. His body could not recover from the accident.

It was the aftermath that killed him.

And as I would cry unrelenting tears of the deepest grief I had ever known to stain the floor of the church where I would sit week after week, I would soon realize that I was drowning too.

That my foundation, my levees, were so depleted and left without strength that surviving the death of a sibling felt impossible. Where was the tap-out button, it was all too much.

Trouble.
Sin.
Death.

This world is full of it.

But "take heart" the Scriptures say, because Jesus has "overcome the world". I had met Jesus as a teenager, but I was about to meet Him in a new way. A way that meant coming in battered clothes and with nothing n my hands. Nothing to give, nothing to show for all of the years I had labored in "good works". Nothing.

If I were the Ugly House my structure would have been completely unrecognizable as a home anymore.

Sometimes it is the unimaginable tragedies that finish us off after the years of small battles we've already been fighting. But God was about to teach me a better way.

personal reflection

1. Take a moment to list out your life as a timeline. What are the highs and lows that mark your life?

2. Where in your story have you been categorically changed? What "big" events have made their mark on you?

3. What small or consistent hardships have helped to shape you? How would you describe their effect on your view of the world and of life?

CHAPTER FOUR

Who Paid the Price?

I waited for my mother in the church parking lot, completely exhausted from the Easter Camp that I had been involved with the week before, and excited to share about my time away.

Her car pulled in, and I smiled. After all these years I am not sure if it was right there before getting in, or maybe upon arriving home, but at some point that day I had embraced my mom and told her that I loved her.

That isn't monumental for you I am sure, but for my mother - it was enough to cause her to sob in relief and exclaim that she felt like she "got her daughter back".

I've shared about my tendencies to cut: the counselor's office and the threat to drive me to a mental institute. I had been struggling for years with anorexia, cutting, suicidal ideation, panic attacks, and such a deep depression that my black clothes were more than a fashion statement and my sullen face had forgotten how to smile.

That "I love you", had been 2 years in the making.

And the smile that extended from one side of my face to the other, was the most genuine thing I had felt since I had my breaking point.

From that point on I would invite anyone who would listen to church, some weeks caravanning 16 students from our home where my parents would make them all dinner and I would tutor them in Math before heading out to youth group on a Wednesday night.

My lifetime dreams of being a math teacher were squashed under the most thrilling knowledge I had ever found... Jesus.

I would never be the same.

I would love to sit and tell you all about the drastic turnaround miracle that the Lord had done in my life, but this book isn't about me. **I am just someone who knows to the depth of my soul that someone bought the Ugly House, the rejected house, the abused house, the overlooked house, and breathed life into it again.**

I don't know why He did it. Why He loves me still, but I can tell you that truly looking into the eyes of a God who sent His Son to die a brutal death to restore a relationship with you that was broken - there will never be enough words to explain how much He paid and how invaluable I had found myself to be.

"You see, at just the right time, when we were still powerless, Christ died for the ungodly. Very rarely will anyone die for a righteous person, though for a good person someone might possibly dare to die. But God demonstrates his own love for us in this: While we were still sinners, Christ died for us." (Romans 5:6-8)

He wasn't paying for the shiny new palace, He put everything on the line for me... a shack. Barely recognizable as a home. And seeing through the span of time, looking at my mistakes and miseries, still chose to give it all.

I cannot fathom this kind of love.

I would be disingenuine if I wrote that I have never let my house get into such a shape again. Just this summer, almost 20 years after meeting Jesus and experiencing the greatest act of freedom that I had ever known, I whispered to my husband late into the night that I was struggling with suicidal thoughts again. I had been for a while. But they were getting louder, and I was too sad to file them away somewhere as they would sit at the forefront of my mind.

I did all of the right things. Made an appointment with my doctor, told a few trusted people, and made sure to eat right and get enough sleep - but when I would sit to pray or spend time alone with God the silence would be Satan's playground for my brain's dysfunction.

Turns out there were a couple of biological things wrong, but also somewhere in the chaos I had let the Builder clean up the back porch and closed the door behind Him thinking I could take charge of the cleaning inside the house.

God was present, He was in my life, but in the depths of my soul where the real battle had been waging - I had excused Him from within those walls.

I had returned to the place that had accepted suffering and torment because I thought that somehow I deserved it. I wasn't even fighting back. I could nod in agreement during every sermon and somehow internalize that the truth was still GOOD and still applied... to everyone else but me. How had I managed to let the Good News of the gospel become "just news" to me?

Jesus' blood did not pay for me to live in anguish. His victory was complete, unchallenged, and unparalleled.

I just needed the reminder to abide with Him. To live with Him and remain in Him. To find my resting place at His feet and in His arms. To know that the most important thing in the house, the only thing that truly mattered, was the one who paid it all to be there. After all, when the Builder bought the Ugly House he didn't set up shop in the garage or down the street in His office - HE MOVED IN. He saw all of the mess and thought it still fitting for a King such as He to wade through the chaos and reside next to His creation.

This was always His intention, His vision for humanity. It is the story of the garden. AW Tozer speaks of our need of God, and only Him, in his book, "The Pursuit of God" when he writes:

> "Before the Lord God made man upon the earth He first prepared for him by creating a world of useful and pleasant things for his sustenance and delight... In the deep heart of the man was a shrine where none but God was worthy to come. Within him was God; without, a thousand gifts which God had showered upon him. But sin has introduced complications and has made those very gifts of God a potential source of ruin to the soul. Our woes

began when God was forced out of His central shrine and 'things' were allowed to enter."[3]

Things are nice but things can never fulfill us or love us like the Builder. The one whom desires us even at our most undesirable.

Being with Him then becomes an easy choice when we recognize that He had already chosen by leaving Heaven to abide with us.

Jesus said to His disciples: "Already you are clean because of the word that I have spoken to you. Abide in me, and I in you. As the branch cannot bear fruit by itself, unless it abides in the vine, neither can you, unless you abide in me. I am the vine; you are the branches. Whoever abides in me and I in him, he it is that bears much fruit, for apart from me you can do nothing." (John 15:3-5)

We all have a tendency to wander. Especially f we are not paying attention. I cannot be the only person that has found themself in auto-pilot going somewhere that I cannot recall but surely am on my way.

Our feet move. Our hearts like to move too.

Abide in the Greek is "menō". It literally means not to depart; to continue to be present; to be held, kept, continually.

Have you ever held a rambunctious puppy? How about one that sees a butterfly while you are trying to leash train them, potentially on a tiny trail on the side of a mountain because you really want them to be your hiking dog? It's terrifying.

There is no understanding of the depth of our downfall to a dog who sees a butterfly. A dog who does not recognize the cliff and certain death looming on the other side. A dog who is frustrated by being held out of reach, while I white knuckle my grip on her leash to keep us both alive.

But that same motion of holding and remaining present reminds me of the word "abide" because it isn't passive. It is active. It is acknowledging that if I were to loosen my attention even for a moment, I would surely be in danger.

It is not fearful, it is secure and unmovable.

Abiding means safety.

I never realized how much body language gives away until doing a deep dive into recognizing when a person feels unsafe. The survival mechanism of fight, flight, or freeze shows up not just in tones or words, but with our bodies. A person in survival mode is not abiding even if they are physically present just like my beloved pet is not abiding when I am holding her back from certain death. I am the one who abides while she attempts her escape because I love her.

Abiding is a recognition and an acceptance of love.

Brother Lawrence wrote in his book "The Practice of the Presence of God": "I consider myself as the most wretched of men, full of sores and corruption, and who has committed all sorts of crimes against his King; touched with a sensible regret, I confess to him all my wickedness, I ask His forgiveness, I abandon myself in His hands that He may do what he pleases with me. The King, full of mercy and goodness, very far from chastising me, embraces me with love, makes me eat at His table, serves me with His own hands, gives me the key of His treasures; He converses and delights Himself with me incessantly, in a thousand and a thousand ways, and treats me in all respects as His favorite. It is thus I consider myself from time to time in His holy presence."[4]

When we live loved, when we recognize the depth of sacrifice that the God of the universe was willing to pay for us not to regain control but out of His care, we choose to stay. When we remember anyway.

That's the real trick isn't it. The distractions and the chaos and the experience of being human can often divert our attentions and our desires away from God. It isn't that we hate God, sometimes we simply forget Him.

Forget His goodness.
Forget His care.

We don't choose another god for ourselves, we simply stop choosing Him and another slips in to take His place.

Surely not me. Not a pastor who had spent the last two decades telling others the Good News. How could I have let my house get so cluttered again? Most spiritual deep thinkers agree. It's easy, actually. It just takes not paying much attention.

So what happens when you do? What happens when you are trying to assess if you've wandered from the Builder? How do you know if in the hustle and bustle, you've pushed Him out?

Stop. Just for a moment. That's how you'll know.

Timothy Keller writes, "An idol is whatever you look at and say, in your heart of hearts, 'If I have that, then I'll feel my life has meaning, then I'll know I have value, then I'll feel significant and secure'... The true god of your heart is what your thoughts effortlessly go to when there is nothing else demanding your attention."[5] **There in the stillness of the pause you will find your answer. That is your god.**

It sounds terrible. How could we? And with such menial things? But still, here we are facing the gods of striving and success and relational security and discontented living. I hate to admit it, but my own thoughts often drift to escaping it all. Perfection was my idol. And when I couldn't attain it, giving up was the next best thing.

Perfection is the greatest lie. It morphs the goodness of God's free gift of salvation into an equateable formula that somehow proves or disproves its validity. It thrusts you onto the ladder of progress while mocking you with words of "never enough". It lets you accept the grace but then holds you hostage to the weight of it until it suffocates you.

Of course, I had left the Builder outside, I was never going to be good enough to feel comfortable with Him living inside the darkest corners of my life.

Distance was safer than feeling the sting of His disapproval. Surely there'd be so much He disapproved of. I had made so much progress but the Guests and Thefts and Hurricanes of Hurt, not to mention my own undoings, had left me feeling more tattered than ever. The longer I lived the messier things somehow got. My best chance was to give Him something to keep Him occupied while I let the real destruction remain hidden. An unimportant task. *Fake bricks.*

God, the gentleman that He is, simply knocked back on the door of my heart to come back inside.

This may be a confusing idea for those who believe that one profession of faith secures eternity for all forever, but that is not what the Scriptures teach. Jesus taught how many will say they knew the Lord from their good works but He will tell them that He never knew them (see Matthew 7). Action isn't proof of salvation.

And even though God will never leave us or forsake us, we can surely leave Him.

Who paid the price for your soul? His name is Jesus Christ, the very Son of God. He loves you with an everlasting love. He died for your sins. The past ones, the present ones, and the future ones.

Repent (make a practice of confessing and turning from your sin... *continually*) and accept the free gift of salvation through Christ. If you don't know how or have never done this, take a moment to pause and pray this next part out loud:

> "God our Father, I believe that out of Your infinite love You have created me. In a thousand ways I have shunned Your love. I repent of each and every one of my sins. Please forgive me. Thank You for sending Your Son to die for me, to save me from eternal death. I choose this day to enter into (renew my) covenant with You and to place Jesus at the center of my heart. I surrender to Him as Lord over my whole life. I ask You now to flood my soul with the gift of the Holy Spirit so that my life may be transformed. Give me the grace and courage to live as a disciple in Your Church for the

rest of my days. Amen." (Taken from the Catholic ministry, St. Paul Street Evangelization.)[6]

When we do this, when we invite Him to live with us, there are times we will be tempted to turn in shame. But we should never assume that Jesus' sacrifice wasn't enough for *this* too. "There is therefore now no condemnation for those who are in Christ Jesus. For the law of the Spirit of life has set you free in Christ Jesus from the law of sin and death." (Romans 8:1-2)

The problem is not our problems, the problem is our response to the sins that God uncovers. The blatant and the hidden ones. Instead of shrieking in terror that we've been found out, or that *something else* exists, what if we were grateful instead? **What if we realized that God was in the work of loving us back to life which means that all signs of death (sin) have to go?**

What if we allowed Him to make us into New Creations and let His Son's blood be enough?

God created you once, and now He is recreating you. It isn't just a restoration project, it is a resurrection one. You aren't getting fixed up, you're being made new.

As the Scriptures say, "Therefore, if anyone is in Christ, he is a new creation. The old has passed away; behold, the new has come. All this is from God, who through Christ reconciled us to himself and gave us the ministry of reconciliation;" (2 Corinthians 5:17-18)

It turns out my mother was right, the Lord did give *all of me* back to her. And while this life still has too many twists and turns for my liking, I will still declare to my weary soul that through Hell and high water - God is with me and within me. He isn't here to visit on weekends, He moved in. He chose me and, as often as He calls out when I wander, I pray that I will continue to choose Him back.

personal reflection

1. When you think of the gospel (or more specifically, what modern believers would call the "Easter Story") what emotions are brought to mind? Does it feel like a real unfolding of history or a work of fiction? Is it more personal or general?

2. In light of your own sins and failures, would you consider Jesus' sacrifice on the cross "enough" to forgive you? Are there any areas that feel too "bad" for God's grace?

PART TWO

sanctification

CHAPTER FIVE

A Mailbox Full

We are, quite literally, turning a page in our journey. Where we spent our first chapters together discussing the condition that the Lord finds us in and His great love that sees all of it and chooses us still, now we are venturing into what life looks like *after* we confess that He is Lord.

This is where things get sticky for a lot of people. Salvation is a beautiful revelation of and response to God's sacrifice to bring us back into a relationship with Him, a story that we so often go back to as we meet new friends in the faith. It is exhilarating and full of joy, even tangible freedom for many. We can't wait to talk about our lives "before" and immediately after Christ. In the church, it is not uncommon to hear in a crowd of acquaintances among the usual ordinary questions of favorites and family breakdowns, "How did you come to faith?" or "How did you meet Jesus?" We love this story!

But the days and weeks and years to follow, we don't get so excited about those. The everyday, mundane, small nuisances or victories get left unsaid. Not once has someone asked, "What is the last thing God has brought you out of?" Or "When did you last experience God's gentle nudge to overcome - by submission - a stubborn area of sin?"

We might actually be uncomfortable with the idea that Christians are still sinners and as such are still undergoing the deep work of what the scriptures call "Sanctification".

Can I let you in on a little secret? Salvation doesn't equal perfection.

The gift of salvation means that Jesus' blood was enough to satisfy the punishment of all sin, and cause us to be reconciled (or made right) with God. A perfect God. But salvation didn't make us perfect. Just forgiven.

And because we weren't remade into perfect beings who make perfect choices, we are still in continual need of Jesus' sacrifice. We are never "good" on our own.

Salvation doesn't set the caged bird free to fly away, however, whenever and wherever it desires. **Salvation sets the caged bird free that has never known how to fly before, and then through the slow work of sanctification, God teaches it how to fly.**

Sanctification is a continual, ongoing act, of *being made* holy by being taught God's ways and will of holiness.

When I was a child my mother would often find me sitting beneath the swing set in our backyard playing in the dirt. This, you might assume, is a usual activity for a small child but as we've come to establish - I have always been a bit unusual.

Upon finding me one day with a bowl of dirt in hand, my mother asked what I had been doing (seriously, it had been hours of just me on the ground in the same place on the dirt. I would start to wonder, too.)

"Purifying dirt," I proudly responded as I drug my fingers through the bowl allowing each grain to fall through my hand.

"What?!" The only natural response, now as a mother I can understand.

"Purifying dirt" I stated more resolute than before.

I had been sitting for multiple hours picking out the larger stones from the soil to make the softest form of sand than one could even imagine. It was tedious work but I never grew tired of it. Because if you could just feel one handful of the new dirt that I had sifted, you would understand. It would make sense and be worth the time it took to separate.

Sanctification is the slow process of God sifting our lives, removing the pangs of sin, and setting us apart for His good work.

But how does He do this? Does it hurt? What might happen when He stumbles upon our faulty neuropathways, gobs of unforgiven offenders, or secretive bad habits and behaviors in His invasive body search? Are we talking accidental metal object in your pocket type of TSA-level discomfort?

Discomfort, sure. His ways are not ours so what God wants will most likely be the furthest thing from our desires at first. But what if we asked more questions about WHO was searching our hearts and less about WHAT He was doing with what He found?

We like to know the process and identify the pain involved, but what about the person?

The pesky metal object in your pocket is way more vomit-inducing when a complete stranger is searching for it, but what if it was your grandmother? How would your grandmother talk to you and look you over? Would she be frowning in disapproval or would kindness fill her eyes as she worked to set you right and on your way?

Please hear me, I am not saying that God is your grandmother. And I am so sorry if you have not experienced the tenderness and love of a doting grandparent. Usually in conversations spanning many cultures, grandparents are the ones noted for their unusual patience and grace so it felt like the natural choice when talking about reframing our vision of God.

God is the vision of patience and grace. And He is also the one who searches our hearts and lives.

David says of Him, "You have searched me, Lord, and you know me. You know when I sit and when I rise; you perceive my thoughts from afar. You discern my going out and my lying down; you are familiar with all my ways." (Psalm 139:1-3)

When we read about an all-knowing God who searches us, we are all bringing into picture who we believe God to be. So ask yourself, how do you see Him? How do you see Him when He is sanctifying (or teaching) you?

What if it feels like a handwritten note from a friend?

Do you want to know what I consider one of the best feelings in the world? Receiving mail. It's true, if I were to open my mailbox and see a letter with my name on it handwritten in ink then undoubtedly you would find me grinning from ear to ear. There is just something about the thoughtfulness and intentionality of a letter that makes holding one so significant.

That feeling is exponentially magnified when it is around a special holiday and grandma has slipped a few dollar bills in the card.

As a grown adult I am still thrilled to see $5 fall to the ground when opening up an envelope around my birthday month. You can't really buy a coffee with that anymore, but you can buy a pint of ice cream and if it is coffee flavored it's basically a two-for-one.

I think that letters like these are the sole reason when moving that people actually fill out the change of address form. That and not wanting their phone service to be turned off. Because all of the junk mail can stay at the old address - no one wants to be followed by a company you submitted your information for entering a giveaway ten years ago. They'll find you none-the-less.

Updating your contact information has come to be a monotonous task. You can move into a house and take up full residence but you still have to prove to the postal service that you're allowed to be there to get the rest of your mail.

So, in essence, having your name listed on the outside of the envelope above the address is proof that you fill the space.

Remember that call to come back to the Ugly House? Well, it has a mailbox too. And the call is not to just come in to see the horrendous state of your body and soul, to have to wade through the aftermath of all of the years of mess that you tried to avoid. The call is to **choose to occupy your life again.** To set up residency because you aren't denying its undesirable state , but instead are choosing to rest in the goodness of the God who chose to stay with you in it still.

And when you move back in, when you make the decision that you have a better chance at living your best life (which has less to do with pursuing happiness and more to do with pursuing God) with a genuine heart that is responding to the love and care of God and not running from the fire of Hell, then guess what, friend? You get mail in your mailbox.

Sure, you might think that you are already able to be reached now. Always. We are forever connected. There are a lot of really great books about the power of disconnecting. But I am not talking about those kinds of messages. The ones with record speed showing up on your doorstep through text messaging and social media ads. The ones that can be heard through the opinions of news anchors and influencers.

Usually, the messages are not sitting in a mailbox for you to come to them, they are banging down your front door. Demanding and provoking feelings of urgency only to be relieved by a quick answer or read to be undaunted by the red bubble that looms over each app calling for attention.

When I say you have mail, **I mean to say that in the slowest and most unpretentious of ways there is a message tucked away with your name on it.**

Snail mail is not chasing you down, it's waiting for you.

And the message, it might be the same one for all believers, but it is still so intentionally personal also for you. As CS Lewis said, *"He died not for men, but for each man. If each man had been the only man made, He would have done no less."*[7]

So here is His message, a small snippet written to the Israelites with the same feelings, thoughts, and intentions He has towards you and me:

> "I have loved you with an everlasting love; I have drawn you with unfailing kindness. I will build you up again..." (Jeremiah 31:3-4)

There it is, the beauty of the sanctifying work that God is doing. The beauty of the message He writes to us in His own handwriting. It isn't *just* a letter, it is a *love* letter with *our* name on it.

Your name, my name. He loves *us*.

How much better is it that we don't just get a coworker out of our relationship with God, we get a companion who loves us through and through? Not just to clean us up and show us off. No, He desires to *build* us up again. To restore us completely. Not out of pity, but out of love. And when we recognize His love for us, it is easy to respond in love to Him.

After all, "We love because he first loved us." (1 John 4:19)

As we journey the road of joining the Builder in the work, what we are really doing is accepting Jesus' act of love in His finished work on the cross for our salvation and partnering with His Spirit in the slow process of sanctification through the reading *and practicing* of His ways.

But there's a caveat...
We can't practice what we don't know.
We can't fix what we don't see as broken.

We have to learn His ways by reading His words. The scriptures are the most impactful way to forge ahead. Jesus Himself showed this to us when He faced off with the devil in the wilderness, responding to each of the tempting taunts with "For it is written."

We have more tools to fight with when we know what was written for us to use.

God did not abandon us to experience this life alone. At any moment, in even the dryest desert of spiritual seasons, we can open the Word of God and declare that "Your love, Lord, reaches to the heavens, your faithfulness to the skies. Your righteousness is like the highest mountains, your justice like the great deep." (Psalm 36: 5-6)

We can sing the Psalms, pray the Psalms, memorize the Psalms, or speak them out loud to encourage those who hear them.

When we need answers, He has them written down for us. Guidance? He tells us to ask Him. **The harrowing adventure that is the life saved and devoted to Him is one of mistakes and rebounds, failures and forgiveness. It is practicing the Way one foot in front of the other, knowing that <u>no one runs down the narrow path.</u>**

Sanctification is slow.

What God is recreating in you, in me, is a masterpiece, and He is taking His time. There is no timeline, no hurry. The slow progress makes us uncomfortable, but for a God who exists outside of time itself, He is not bothered by our inexpedience - just our commitment to Him.

So keep going. Rise again. Throw off the weight of expectations and allow yourself to be in the exact shape that you are. Let God step into the framework of your life as it exists, not as you want it to be.

"For the word of God is alive and active. Sharper than any double-edged sword, it penetrates even to dividing soul and spirit, joints and marrow; it judges the thoughts and attitudes of the heart. Nothing in all creation is hidden from God's sight. Everything is uncovered and laid bare before the eyes of him to whom we must give account." (Hebrews 4:12-13)

He is not going to be surprised at its state. You are just going to have to risk the embarrassment of facing what He already knows. And even then, there is beauty in what God can do with the rubble. (Just read Romans 8:28!)

Sin entered with the sting of shame in the garden, but Christ has defeated that. Shame gets to go back to the depths of Hell where it came from as we, the forgiven, walk out the reconciling of every part of our lives back to the fullness of God by the victory that Jesus purchased with His blood.

This is what our Bible says. **This is a love letter.**

Open and read. Or as David says in Psalm 34:8 - "Taste and see that the Lord is good; blessed is the one who takes refuge in him."

personal reflection

1. When you imagine God while reading the scriptures or talking to Him in prayer, who are you picturing? What is His countenance and character?

2. Would it be difficult for you to imagine someone as perfect justice and all-merciful?

3. What is the biggest hurdle you have when engaging with God? How might you reframe that challenge to desire getting to know Him more?

CHAPTER SIX

Locks and the Key

As the fall of 2016 came roaring to an end for our family, and I do mean roaring in every sense of a lioness rage, we found ourselves in the midst of a seemingly unending sabbatical after burying two family members all the while navigating the exciting life of RV-living in a church parking lot of a town we'd never been in before. I understand that many people choose the RV life, but this wasn't such the case for us. It was just where the Lord had brought us. And I would be amiss if I didn't share that it was the biggest leap of faith I had ever made due to there being a perfectly good house 2 hours away that we were still paying rent for... but God had asked us to volunteer. Here. Now. All together.

We had a lot of highs and lows in that RV. Thankfully with two young boys, it was parked in a beautiful place and offered mostly good weather. We watched the presidential election in that RV. Started preschool for my youngest son in that RV. And even hosted visits in that RV. If it's not the most awkward thing in all of the world to invite someone over for coffee only for them to realize that you are giving them the church address and inviting them into the giant motor home parked out in front. The only more awkward thing is that while we had electricity, we did not have water, so anytime we needed to cook or use the facilities - we headed into the church.

The folding tables in the multipurpose room became our dining area and the multi-stall bathrooms became the place we would get dressed. It was obviously very glamorous.

One night when it was torrential down pouring enough to break a few records, my son woke me up in a panic because all of that water must have brainwashed him into needing to use the restroom at 3 am. We jetted out the door and into the floodgates, clenching our jackets and each other closely. We got to the door and I inserted the key but I couldn't get it to turn. I jiggled it and did all of the usual motions that a person at 3 am would think to do in the rain with a newly-potty trained toddler and still no luck. I must have taken it in and out a few times before my brain slowly came to me and I remembered that the key was a little short. The trick was not to push it in all of the ways before turning it slightly to the left. Somehow just being "similar enough" was enought for the door to unlock.

This is not great for business but with an old church that had those front door keys duplicated and handed out to a good many dozen pastors, janitors, and members over the years, it was no surprise that it wasn't a good fit anymore. But it was "good enough".

We still entered and were able to do what we came for.

Good enough was good enough for me.

We've been at this church for a good many years now and those front doors still give us trouble. We finally found the right master key and have since paired down on the imposters but there are still a few floating around. I know because I get to watch as some do the same song and dance I had done all those years ago. And the door, well the face of the lock is scratched and battered from all of the frustrated attempts at getting inside. We'll be replacing it sooner rather than later, if not for it breaking down altogether then for sure for safety.

We only lock things we wish to protect. Because they are important to us. We know the value that they hold and we don't want just anyone with a counterfeit key and malintent to barge on in.

But if I had cared about my heart as much as I had cared about that church, I might have found myself in a better place at 37 years old.

The scriptures say "Above all else, guard your heart, for everything you do flows from it." (Proverbs 4:23)

That's kind of a big deal when the scriptures, especially one of the books of wisdom, put something above everything else. But there it is, God instructs us to *guard* our hearts.

Have you ever observed a guard? Anything from a basketball player to the soldiers who stand in front of the king's palace in England. They are pretty fascinating to watch.

The intensity on their face, the resolute posture of their bodies, the laser focus in their eyes, the way they move to oppose every forward advance. They are committed to the job. *But why?* They find great value in what they are guarding.

Like the lock on our front doors, a guard is intended to meet every visitor to weigh out their worthiness and the intention of their entry.

Have we ever been so careful with our own lives?

While we imagine ourselves to be this valuable Dream House that the Maker pours His life over, are we also placing value in this home? Do we call it worthy? Do we find it is something to guard? Like the home that was still being worked on was locked to protect the progress being made, do we find that because we haven't reached perfection and completion yet that our door can just stay open to anyone who might want to come in?

Here is the truth, **every one of us needs a lock on our doors.**

Not to shut everyone out, but to create a boundary that allows for us to choose who or what comes in or stays out of our hearts and minds. That isn't un-Christian. God made it pretty clear through Paul's writings that there are to be boundaries with our human relationships when he penned 2 Corinthians 6:14: "Do not be yoked together with unbelievers. For what do righteousness and wickedness have in common? Or what fellowship can light have with darkness?"

A yoking together wasn't just sharing a meal, it was a committed partnership. A deep connection that caused you to share life and all of it's burdens with one another. This kind of companionship is impossible to share with those who see the very fundamental truths differently.

What advice would you be given if you started working and not taking a Sabbath?

Or felt too tired to attend church on Sundays?
Or started gossiping about others in the workplace?
Or were betrayed by a friend or loved one?

The truth is that someone who does not believe the scriptures to be the inspired Word of a loving God for you would not say that the Sabbath was a gift for your body and greatly important for your emotional/spiritual/physical health. Nor would they say that not coming together with other believers would hinder your growth and desire for the Lord, or that speaking of others would only cause harm to your relationships. And surely it would be madness for them to speak that forgiveness would set your own heart free from the bondage of offense.

Our words and the words communicated back to us, matter. They are the very key to this life.

"From the fruit of their mouth a person's stomach is filled; with the harvest of their lips they are satisfied. The tongue has the power of life and death, and those who love it will eat its fruit." (Proverbs 18:20-21)

"What goes into someone's mouth does not defile them, but what comes out of their mouth, that is what defiles them." (Matthew 15:11)

Words.

I have heard it said that "our words create our world" and it is true. We are not the Creator who quite literally spoke and the world was created, but how we speak of ourselves, others, or our situations helps to define how we respond and interact with each. And the continual enforcement of that spoken word, that belief, will shape our lives.

For better or worse.
For life or death.
So what does it look like to guard our hearts and watch our words?

It looks a lot like a house with a lock and a key.

We guard our heart by choosing that we are not just opening ourselves up to anything and everything this world offers up. It looks like boundaries or defined expectations or communicated vision and purpose. This is our lock.

It hangs on the door of our heart and reminds us that whomever or whatever shows up at our door (*hello Amazon packages*), we still get to continue to choose the worthiness and intention of that moment.

And we open it with the key.

Our "yes" opens the door. Our own spoken agreement that anything on the other side of that door has direct access to our hearts.

If we are honest with ourselves we would know that we too have used a lot of ill-fitting keys that got the job done but left a little damage behind. Saying yes when we should have said no. Speaking harshly to ourselves when we should have spoken gently. *Sometimes we are our biggest bully.*

But we don't get to play this thing backwards. We are living in the here and now so no matter the state of the house or the line of losers that you've had at the front door, locks can be replaced. Keys can be changed out.

If you've allowed access or given permission in the past, you can use the same tools to change that now. Your words.

Your words will shape the world you live in, but that doesn't mean the world can't change. You can start fresh today.

"If you declare with your mouth, 'Jesus is Lord,' and believe in your heart that God raised him from the dead, you will be saved. For it is with your heart that you believe and are justified, and it is with your mouth that you profess your faith and are saved." (Romans 10:9-10)

"Therefore, if anyone is in Christ, he is a new creation. The old has passed away; behold, the new has come." (2 Corinthians 5:17)

Just like that.

Our words confess our faith in Christ and upon that declaration, we are made new. Continually.

If you used a bad key the day before, look around and find the right one for today. Let your words reflect His Word and watch how your life will flourish.

personal reflection

1. What words have you uttered that you need to ask forgiveness for? What gossip have you entered into or agreements have you made that have not reflected your identity as a son or daughter of God, deeply loved by their Father?

2. What words have been spoken over you that need to be surrendered for God to rewrite your identity, vision, or purpose?

God called

you a ~~good~~

creation

CHAPTER SEVEN

The Most Secure System

Living in post-Y2K America is pretty wild most days. We have more access to everything always and yet there is this steady decline in happiness and overall well-being. We've reduced rooms full of computer software to devices that we can now fit inside of a pocket in our pants. We're connected, tethered even, and yet the most disconnected generation that ever lived.

Walking around most days you will see the majority of people with their phones in their hands. What are we doing? How long do we imagine that we can live this way? Is this really living?

I have questions, but they aren't rage against the machine - stick it to the man - kind of ponderings. They feel more likened to walking around in a dream and feeling that eerie sensation where you know no one is really awake. You could be in your underwear and no one would actually even notice.

Or they would and would plaster it all over the internet for you to never recover from.

We have given so much of our own power to a device that is never getting powered down.

Pick your vice of choice - Instagram, X, Snapchat, TikTok (the list will surely be unending and many more will undoubtedly be added). What are we even grasping for while we scroll?

The two year old inside of me never actually got over the questioning phase. It might be one of my best qualities, I think. Because I am always asking "why".

Why am I here?
Why did I respond with so much angst?
Why is the natural instinct to pick up our phones?
Why am I pouring a third cup of coffee?

I know the answer to that last one - *looking at you sleepless toddler* - but the rest of the list? At any given moment the answer might be different. And it turns out that even having lived every day as myself, I actually truly know very little about who I am.

I am complicated. I can't even figure me out.

So we grab our phones or our friends or some coping mechanism that we've developed to help fill in the gaps.

I am not anti-technology. It is such a useful tool. But it is not a mind reader or a life definer, despite being asked to be both.

If we are to build our lives with the Lord, then we must be sure that the good plans aren't thwarted or tainted in some way by recognizing who we've given authority to give their input. Our words may be keeping people and things in or out of our doors but if there is some Instagram influencer or YouTuber who is kept on repeat in your life - then don't be surprised when you start speaking the way they do, holding to the ideologies they share, or behaving towards others in the same likeness as they've acted.

We liken our lives to who we listen to.

And friends, they don't know God's good plans for your life. Don't build someone else's dream home. Don't live someone else's life.

When we first moved across town while I was approximately 47 years pregnant with our first son, we were excited to see that the new house had a security system due to their being a faulty swamp cooler in our previous rental. How did I know? Because there was a sign so of course they had one.

We were blessed because a security system wasn't a make-or-break amenity in our otherwise low-crime middle-class suburban track home neighborhood, but when you are thinking about bringing a fresh baby into the world (being a baby yourself) the added safety of a security system feels like the right place to start. It wasn't just me devoted to protecting my child, the whole house was going to be on watch.

When we unpacked that next day (because this is who I am as a person), and started hanging pictures on day 2, I thought a great project to tackle on the third day while waiting for my son to come was to look into setting the notifications to alert our phones should something happen at the house.

I called the number on the sign and was abruptly told that the security system was no longer active in the home. And it was going to take a monthly subscription that I had imagined was included in our rent, but was not, to reactivate it.

I was facing the upcoming arrival of our child whom I had heard would be the most expensive investment we would ever make and the drastically reduced income while I stayed home the first few years so I did what any new mother would do, I left the sign up.

If I couldn't pay for the service, I could at least pretend that we had a system to ward off the potential ill-intentioned thieves from considering our house an easy target.

I am not saying that this won't work. I have come to find out that it is more common than we know. With the rise of accessible security systems and advanced technology, there are still some who would rather have the sign than the real thing. **It is cheaper to have a sign than an ongoing service.**

Until someone breaks in, then there would have been no price too high to pay to protect my family. *Fingers crossed no one actually tested if we were covered or not.*

Looking back this is a bit of a terrifying way to live. "Fingers crossed." It is basically saying to the universe that you are willingly ignoring that threats exist. I don't want to live in fear of constant threats - but I am also not naive to the idea of crime happening to unsuspecting victims.

It's the unsuspecting part that gives it away. No one actually sees it coming.

And if someone is breaking in I need a real agency to call my house to warn me of the danger and to send the police to check on us, not a sign to wave in my face that I had trusted in some faulty hopeful thinking.

There is too much at stake. This house holds not just possessions that are valuable, but souls of immeasurable value. And it is the same with the house that the Builder is building with us. The work is too valuable, *we* are too valuable.

Wearing a shirt or hanging a frame with a verse won't make the truths of scripture embed deep into your heart.

Listening to Christian music won't make the words of your mouth come out as edifying and encouraging to the world around you.

Attending church services won't get your name written into the book of life.

There are things that we cling to that have become nothing more than empty signs to give us a faulty sense of security that we are "doing ok". As if doing well were the point. But how are you really? How is your soul?

In all of the chaos of this life there is a peace that surpasses understanding and it isn't just something we talk about as if some superbreed of Christians are the only ones to experience it. But how do we internalize this gift from God and live as kingdom people? How do we live as children of God, loved back to life into a new family?

We call the security system, and we offer the cost it takes to turn it back on.

In scripture, it says that Jesus left His disciples in an Upper Room after being with them post His resurrection for 40 days. What were they waiting for? Him. But also a Him they had not known.

God is a trinitarian being, He exists in three persons as one God. He is Father, Son, and Spirit. They had known Him as their Father, they had met the Son, and they might have experienced glimpses of the Spirit - but they were about to experience God and what it meant to be a follower of Jesus Christ in a brand new way.

They waited, together, in the Upper Room. Shoulder to shoulder, expectantly hopeful, that a gift from God would appear.

Can you imagine the rumblings of what those gathered might have been saying? What ideas or hypotheses were shared as to who or what they were waiting for? All that they were left with was that they had to wait because the Helper was better than Jesus Himself.

Jesus their Messiah.
Jesus their Savior.
Jesus their Friend.

This was going to be better.

As they waited in patient expectancy, God met them in a new way. Their old understandings of God taught to them in the temple and around tables were about to be met with a new embodied experience like none other than they had experienced before. Their security systems were turned on.

In scripture the Spirit of God is referred to as many things in the life of a believer - our strength (Acts 1:8), help (ever present), teacher (teach you in all things), and guide (conviction). The usefulness of God coming to reside in our home goes well beyond a master architect that is restoring furniture. He wants to restore *everything* back to life.

That is what Jesus paid for on the cross. **He didn't get resuscitated - He was resurrected.**

He was dead for three days - and then He was alive **as if it had never happened.**

God is not just resuscitating our dry bones, He is breathing on them back to life as if they had never known the darkness and pains of death.

And while the believers until this moment had to wait for moments in time that God would meet them, this was going to be something new. This was going to be an always present, always working, always guiding kind of relationship with the Lord. We weren't getting visitations anymore, we were getting embodiment. And it was going to be better than we ever imagined.

But there is a price.

What is the cost of the Spirit of God indwelling inside of you, the temple? First, it took Jesus' life.

In order for us to be completely redeemed and purchased back - the punishment of our sin covered in full - Jesus had to die. Sin always leads to death, and accepting Jesus into our lives means accepting that His death is enough for our restoration. He paid the price.

"Or do you not know that your body is a temple of the Holy Spirit within you, whom you have from God? You are not your own, for you were bought with a price. So glorify God in your body". (1 Corinthians 6:20)

That is what Jesus did, but what does it cost us? He already did His part but that doesn't mean we will get to have what He paid for. We have to receive it. We have to call out to Him and invite Him in.

"Jesus said to him, 'I am the way, and the truth, and the life. No one comes to the Father except through me'." (John 14:6)

The first disciples had accepted Jesus' life and death, and by all accounts had followed the Way. So what did it take for them to receive the gift of the Spirit? Patience... and submission.

They weren't just waiting with arms folded and hearts hardened, they were gathered together in one spirit and with expectancy for the God of the universe to meet them. And when a king walks into a room (this sounds like the start to a bad joke) no one stands. **There is a reverence for their presence** because of who they are in contrast to who you are. The submissive ones bow. The ones with authority are raised up.

This imagery is really important because it says that God, Creator of the heavens and the earth, doesn't just leave us as slaves. He isn't walking by for us to worship as though we were some lowly creature, banished from His perfect world. He loves us that He gave everything to be reconciled back to us, to purchase us back into His kingdoms not as slaves but as sons and daughters. He isn't holding His authority over our heads in an abusive and prideful way,

He is actually desiring to share it with all of us. To partner in the work of reconciliation of the world.

We get to be co-workers with the King Himself

We should have been slaves, we deserved to be banished, but God redeemed us to rule and reign with H m. But we're not equal.

We both hold that we have some authority but *not all* authority. That we are leaders *and* servants. We are in the king's court but *we are not the king*. The throne is not for us.

When we are sleeping, He is not.
When we are worrying, He is not.
When we are struggling to understand the way forward, He is not.

The cost of the security system is our giving up our own pride and positioning our hearts in submission to God. Throughout scripture, we are instructed to wait on God and to obey His words. This is not because He is a tyrant, He is simply the rightful King. And we are getting the better end of the deal. Seriously, have you met humans? Have you read about how humans have ruled throughout the centuries?

We were never intended to take His place.

God desires to bring all of His power and authority to your house. But if He comes it means He sits in the place of power and authority over our own hearts first.

He gets to make the rules. He gets to make the grand plans. But He also gets to be the one who guards and protects the work. Which is great news, because He doesn't take a day off and He works nights.

His Spirit inside of you means living with power and submission, courage and conviction. **It means that you're covered and that, when you are in danger, help is not just coming - it is here.**

Of course, we don't always know what He is saying or doing. But I can assure you that if a fire started in my house, I wouldn't be asking too many critical questions of the firemen who show up. I could guarantee that they would know more than I would. And the same is true of the Lord, He isn't just the Builder - He is the Helper, and He knows everything.

When I am with Him, when I recognize that He is with me, then I get to be the dumb sheep. As David says, "The Lord is my shepherd, I lack nothing. He makes me lie down in green pastures, he leads me beside quiet waters, he refreshes my soul. He guides me along the right paths for his name's sake." (Psalm 23:1-3)

The sheep doesn't know what to do or where to go, but the Shepherd does. How silly would it be to see a sheep revolt and claim their way was better? (Actually, it happens. Animals are just as silly as we are.)

The Shepherd still leads and guides. It is not just His responsibility, it is His joy. And God's Spirit being poured out into our lives means that we get constant access to the One who knows the way. Even if we only get to see the step right in front of us because He also knows the sheep who might get too overwhelmed with the whole path.

One day at a time. One step at a time. The Lord works in our lives. In His goodness to us He didn't just leave us a love letter to try and decipher on our own, He left us a Helper to apply it to our lives. To lead us in paths of righteousness for His name's sake.

AW Tozer says of His speaking: "That God is here and that He is speaking - these truths are back of all other Bible truths; without them there could be no revelation at all. God did not write a book and send it by messenger to be read at a distance by unaided minds. He spoke a Book and lives in His spoken words, constantly speaking His words and causing the power of them to persist across the years." [8]

His role is to speak, and ours is to (from a place of deep regard and desire for the Lord) listen and obey.

It isn't a matter of "having to", it is a soul's response to the unveiled love of God to them personally that moves their heart into "wanting to."

As we get to know Him better, we trust and love and heed His voice more. Because the reigning King has become our friend.

personal reflection

1. What is your natural response to the feeling of conviction?

2. How might you put into practice reframing conviction from a shameful experience to one of helpful leading into a healthier place out of love?

3. Where have you desired to take authority back and need to surrender back to the Lord?

PSALMS
TO
pray

ninety one

1 Whoever dwells in the shelter of the Most High
will rest in the shadow of the Almighty.
2 I will say of the Lord, "He is my refuge and my fortress,
my God, in whom I trust."
3 Surely he will save you
from the fowler's snare
and from the deadly pestilence.
4 He will cover you with his feathers,
and under his wings you will find refuge;
his faithfulness will be your shield and rampart.
5 You will not fear the terror of night,
nor the arrow that flies by day,
6 nor the pestilence that stalks in the darkness,
nor the plague that destroys at midday.
7 A thousand may fall at your side,
ten thousand at your right hand,
but it will not come near you.
8 You will only observe with your eyes
and see the punishment of the wicked.
9 If you say, "The Lord is my refuge,"
and you make the Most High your dwelling,
10 no harm will overtake you,
no disaster will come near your tent.
11 For he will command his angels concerning you
to guard you in all your ways;
12 they will lift you up in their hands,
so that you will not strike your foot against a stone.
13 You will tread on the lion and the cobra;
you will trample the great lion and the serpent.
14 "Because he loves me," says the Lord, "I will rescue him;
I will protect him, for he acknowledges my name.
15 He will call on me, and I will answer him;
I will be with him in trouble,
I will deliver him and honor him.
16 With long life I will satisfy him
and show him my salvation."

sixteen

1 Keep me safe, my God,
for in you I take refuge.
2 I say to the Lord, "You are my Lord;
apart from you I have no good thing."
3 I say of the holy people who are in the land,
"They are the noble ones in whom is all my delight."
4 Those who run after other gods will suffer more and more.
I will not pour out libations of blood to such gods
or take up their names on my lips.
5 Lord, you alone are my portion and my cup;
you make my lot secure.
6 The boundary lines have fallen for me in pleasant places;
surely I have a delightful inheritance.
7 I will praise the Lord, who counsels me;
even at night my heart instructs me.
8 I keep my eyes always on the Lord.
With him at my right hand, I will not be shaken.
9 Therefore my heart is glad and my tongue rejoices;
my body also will rest secure,
10 because you will not abandon me
to the realm of the dead,
nor will you let your faithful one see decay.
11 You make known to me the path of life;
you will fill me with joy in your presence,
with eternal pleasures at your right hand.

1 You have searched me, Lord, and you know me.

2 You know when I sit and when I rise; you perceive my thoughts from afar.

3 You discern my going out and my lying down; you are familiar
with all my ways.

4 Before a word is on my tongue you, Lord, know it completely.

5 You hem me in behind and before, and you lay your hand upon me.

6 Such knowledge is too wonderful for me, too lofty for me to attain.

7 Where can I go from your Spirit? Where can I flee from your presence?

8 If I go up to the heavens, you are there; if I make my bed
in the depths, you are there.

9 If I rise on the wings of the dawn, if I settle on the far side of the sea,

10 even there your hand will guide me, your right hand will hold me fast.

11 If I say, "Surely the darkness will hide me and the light become
night around me,"

12 even the darkness will not be dark to you; the night will shine
like the day, for darkness is as light to you.

13 For you created my inmost being; you knit me together
in my mother's womb.

14 I praise you because I am fearfully and wonderfully made;
your works are wonderful, I know that full well.

15 My frame was not hidden from you when I was made in the secret place,
when I was woven together in the depths of the earth.

16 Your eyes saw my unformed body; all the days ordained for me were
written in your book before one of them came to be.

17 How precious to me are your thoughts, God! How vast is the sum of them!

18 Were I to count them, they would outnumber the grains of sand—
when I awake, I am still with you.

19 If only you, God, would slay the wicked! Away from me,
you who are bloodthirsty!

20 They speak of you with evil intent; your adversaries misuse your name.

21 Do I not hate those who hate you, Lord, and abhor those
who are in rebellion against you?

22 I have nothing but hatred for them; I count them my enemies.

23 Search me, God, and know my heart; test me
and know my anxious thoughts.

24 See if there is any offensive way in me,
and lead me in the way everlasting.

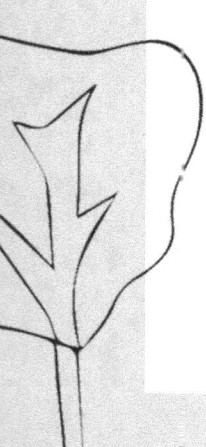

twenty three

1 The Lord is my shepherd, I lack nothing.
2 He makes me lie down in green pastures,
he leads me beside quiet waters,
3 he refreshes my soul. He guides me along
the right paths for his name's sake.
4 Even though I walk through the darkest valley,
I will fear no evil, for you are with me; your rod
and your staff, they comfort me.
5 You prepare a table before me in the presence of my enemies.
You anoint my head with oil; my cup overflows.
6 Surely your goodness and love will follow me all the days of my
life, and I will dwell in the house of the Lord forever.

four

1 Answer me when I call to you, my righteous God. Give me relief
from my distress; have mercy on me and hear my prayer.
2 How long will you people turn my glory into shame?
How long will you love delusions and seek false gods?
3 Know that the Lord has set apart his faithful servant for
himself; the Lord hears when I call to him.
4 Tremble and do not sin; when you are on your beds,
search your hearts and be silent.
5 Offer the sacrifices of the righteous and trust in the Lord.
6 Many, Lord, are asking, "Who will bring us prosperity?"
Let the light of your face shine on us.
7 Fill my heart with joy when their grain and new wine abound.
8 In peace I will lie down and sleep, for you alone, Lord,
make me dwell in safety.

CHAPTER EIGHT

Fences for Good Futures

When we moved into the parsonage of the church that we now pastor on the Central Coast, the previous pastors noted that we would need to be careful when letting the children play outside. The house was built on the side of a hill and just on the other side of our fenceline was a 20-foot drop. When looking out you wouldn't notice it much. Actually, it was pretty great because it meant the houses below ours couldn't obstruct the view of the mountain that would give me the greatest sense of peace each morning upon waking when I would see it out of our windows.

A house on a hill - it is basically biblically perfect.

And because I love being outdoors, it didn't take long for me to venture outside with our two boys to find some kind of adventure.

The best part of the yard was this tree growing next to the fence. I love trees. Greenery of all kinds really. And this fully grown tree offered the greatest shade to be able to sit and enjoy the yard. Outside. Where I love.

But having been married to my husband for some time now it didn't take long for the plan of cutting down the tree to be presented. WHO DOESN'T LOVE TREES??

I watched him rip out bushes and vegetation every opportunity he could get and knew my beloved tree would make the list one day but I was ready to stand my ground. Not this tree. Not on my watch.

Now before you go and think that my husband is some kind of planet-killer, there really were a few good reasons for his other decisions. One was dying, a few were ill-planted in shallow ground, and the trees that were pruned to look like bony fingers reaching up from the earth just around the fall time when things get spooky anyway (I really wish I was kidding) were purely for them to grow in a more symmetrical way. But still, who wants to come home to knobby wood stumps reaching out from the ground like all of the scary stories told to you as a child?

When cutting my tree was presented I immediately went into the defense... and then I was led to the tree that I loved and told to look at its roots.

It was planted just next to the fence (making it all the better in my book as we would get the most use of the yard) but due to the grade on the other side of our property, had nowhere to grow but under our fenceline. I reached out to the fence that was keeping my children in our yard and not tumbling down the 20-foot embankment on the other side and realized why it was so important to tell us about the backyard that day.

Our fence was shaky.

You would never notice it because it was still standing and could take a ball or two being thrown at it without the slightest movement, but if either of my children were to put their whole weight into it I shudder to think what might have happened.

My once strong opinions about the beauty of our yard being preserved took a drastic left turn because **what had once been an image of rest and strength, was now the very thing putting our whole family at risk.**

And I might never have even noticed it.

Fences. They are only as helpful as they are secure.

When I imagine the house that God is building and the basic criteria of the work being kept protected, I think of fences. Think of it - before something new is even started to be constructed the first thing you always see is a fence. It is a sign of taking control of the land, protecting the process.

They are more than just a symbol telling us what we are responsible for and what is someone else's. They are also a sign for others to know when they are entering our homes.

A fence is a boundary.

The ugly house had a fence, it was one of the first things the Builder did as He took back what was used and abused to the undoing of our friend. It kept her on the outside for a while until she was brave enough to cross its threshold. But she did make it back inside. It was a good fence, a true fence, but there are many kinds of fences that could have been built.

The No Trespassing Fence

The one that is tall and intimidating, created to prevent anyone or anything from entering. It is always this kind of fence that makes me want to peer inside the most. Not because I am rebellious, but because the house behind it is intentionally kept hidden. Which only makes my mind wander into stories of forbidden castles and locked-away princesses. Why hide? What joy can be found in shutting the whole world out?

The Wide Open Fence

This one is always a hoot because it is merely for show. If your fence is wide enough for a child to fit under, an adult to step over, a raccoon to crawl through, or a dog to escape, then the fence is only a pencil drawing of what you are managing and nothing more. It is the polar opposite of the No Trespassing fence that aims to keep everyone out, this Wide Open Fence is inviting anyone and anything in. Your doormat might as well read "My house is your house".

The Broken Fence

While the last one might make a person scratch their head, a broken fence leaves no such room for such wonder. Something has happened here. Something tragic and hurtful. Whether all in good fun, accidentally done, or with the worst of intentions... broken fences mean costly repairs.

The Shakey Fence

This one is the sneakiest of all because, like our own backyard, there is a perception of safety and security. The assumption is that all is well and nothing is amiss. And yet should a tragedy occur, you would beat yourself up with the "shoulda knowns" forever. When we never inspect the fence, never look at the encroaching threats masked as desirable things, we never know what danger we are truly in. We never know until we are faced with the pain of knowing.

The Secure Fence

The Builder knew what He was doing when He built a secure Fence around the Ugly House. It kept threats out and guests playfully in. It wasn't built near any desirable dangers and could weather the storms for years to come. Knowing it would need attention from time to time, the tools were still kept readily available. *No fence is forever.* But it was doing its job.

The job of preserving the sacred work.

A boundary (or fence) exists to preserve, and when it comes to our lives what is being preserved is the work of God in us and through us.

God rightfully gives us boundaries to declare what is within our responsibility to manage. We can think of this as Adam in the Garden of Eden when the scriptures say "The Lord God took the man and put him in the garden of Eden to work it and keep it." (Genesis 2:15). The garden was Adam's responsibility to "work" and "keep".

But the garden had a boundary. How do we know that? When Adam and Eve disobeyed God's instructions by eating of the Tree of Knowledge of Good and Evil, they had to leave. **You can only leave something that is established by a boundary line.**
And **a boundary only makes sense when there are guidelines in which to behave to stay within its borders.**
If it didn't matter, then Adam and Eve could have sinned and nothing would have changed. But instead, God shows

us that they were removed from the garden (*see Genesis 3:23-24*).

We would naturally think that they were removed as punishment - to give them a glimpse of perfection for them to remember their shame as they painfully labored for the rest of their lives.

Scriptures do not speak of their shame. In fact, God does the opposite. God covers them with grace.

How might I make that conclusion knowing full well that due to their rebellion, we all lost privileges to the garden?

It happens just before their exile.

When they were naked and hiding from their shame, clothing themselves with leaves that were sure to dry and crumble, God met them and told them of the consequences of their choice. The one He warned them of from the beginning. And, being able to leave it at "they knew what would happen", *still* clothed them with a garment that would never fade away.

"21 And the Lord God made for Adam and for his wife garments of skins and clothed them. 22 Then the Lord God said, 'Behold, the man has become like one of us in knowing good and evil. Now, lest he reach out his hand and take also of the tree of life and eat, and live forever—' 23 therefore the Lord God sent him out from the garden of Eden to work the ground from which he was taken. 24 He drove out the man, and at the east of the garden of Eden he placed the cherubim and a flaming sword that turned every way to guard the way to the tree of life." (Genesis 3:21-24)

Did you notice how God clothed them? With the skin of an animal. And because we understand that animals aren't skinned alive, this means that something had to die in order for their sin and shame to be eternally covered. **Sin requires death.**

God's grace is Jesus Christ.

And God's love is in the changed boundary lines.

They were in the wrong. They disobeyed. But their disobedience was only the beginning of what could have put all of humanity at even more risk. If they couldn't honor God's boundary with the Tree of Knowledge, how could they be trusted with such close proximity to the Tree of Life?

There is a deep dive here into the difference between the trees, but to overly simplify for the sake of keeping on focus - partaking of the Tree of Knowledge meant bringing sin and death to earth (see Genesis 2:17, Romans 5:12, Romans 5:19), partaking in the tree of life meant a final state of death that could never be redeemed through Jesus Christ.

It was that serious. They had to be banished. But the plan was never to keep them out forever... God sent Jesus, Jesus was our ultimate sacrifice to pay the penalty of our sin (death) so that we could be in right standing with God again, and dwell with Him forever. The ultimate restoration. **Their distance was to preserve the end goal of their reconciliation.**

And this is where this chapter comes to its conclusion, with the purpose of the fence.

A fence is not too tall to keep everyone out.

A fence is not too minimal to let everyone in.
A fence is not to be given up on when broken.
A fence is not to be unattended and assumed fine.
A fence is to preserve the good work.

Now replace the fence with boundaries, which are what this chapter hopes to relate to our lives.
Our boundaries with others are not to be:
Too big to keep everyone out.
Too small to let everyone in.
Given up on when broken.
Or, left unattended and assumed as fine.

Our boundaries are our intentional relational borders that preserve the good work of loving God and loving people.

They are not punishment for other's bad behavior, but instead a reflection of the closest we can be to someone to love ourselves and others best. Meaning, boundaries are really all about love.

Lysa Terkeurst in her book *"Good Boundaries and Goodbyes"* puts it this way, "Boundaries aren't meant to shove love away. Quite the opposite. We set boundaries so we know what to do when we very much want to love those around us really well without losing ourselves in the process. Good boundaries help us preserve the love within us even when some relationships become unsustainable and we must accept the reality of a goodbye."[9]

Boundaries mean setting parameters in our relationships with others *to* love them. But unfortunately for some who are used to manipulating, lying, abusing, or disregarding others - keeping that fence gate closed is the best way to love them. Distance doesn't mean hate, just like Adam and

Eve being removed from the garden didn't mean eternal damnation. Love is safe and when it is unsafe, distance gives space to grow toward healing... with or without the other person.

To preserve the work that God is doing inside of you, the work of His Spirit to build you into a Holy Temple, a beautiful palace, will take intentional efforts of preservation.

It will mean assessing the proximity of your relationships and asking hard questions.

Who have you let in?
Who have you given full access to?
Who have you been keeping out without a plan of forgiveness or repentance?

If God is love (1 John 4:8), the fruit of His Spirit is love (Galatians 5:22), the greatest commandment is love (Matthew 22:27-28), and our confirmation of being a disciple is by our love (John 13:35)... then having boundaries is vital to the mission.

Because being a follower of Jesus Christ means loving the world that God made in His image in the way that God loved them... with boundaries.

So here is the measuring stick: love.
And here is the question: was this boundary created to preserve my love *for* others or protect me *from* others?

Our starting point is either love or fear but it is never both. You have chosen, but you can choose again. My dear friend, this time, choose love.

"There is no fear in love, but perfect love casts out fear. For fear has to do with punishment, and whoever fears has not been perfected in love. We love because he first loved us." (1 John 4:18-19)

personal reflection

1. Have you established boundaries in your life? Were they created out of fear to protect your heart or to love others the best from the responding distance?

2. What boundary have you created that might need to be adjusted?

3. Which boundaries might need to be created or reinstated to preserve the work God is doing in your life?

CHAPTER NINE

Good Guard Dogs

My parents adopted a Chihuahua while vacationing at the beach with my younger siblings many years ago. I never had time to bond with the dog and what was even more unfortunate was that they loved it so much. It was just hard to be welcomed into their home with a constantly barking floor-wetter.

In his defense, the peeing happened in his older years but I may or may not have still mumbled "Hello *PeePee*" instead of his real name, "Petey" every time I would visit.

As much flack as I gave that dog, he was a good companion to my parents, and if his job was to prevent people from wanting to enter the house, he was doing it. Never mind that I am their child, and even after 17 years, he was still trying to thwart my attempts at coming in.

There are a lot of different kinds of pet owners in this world but my favorite thing to dissect is the purpose for why people do what they do - which includes owning a pet.

If you want a friend, then the dog is usually sleeping in your bed and licking your face every morning with some "huffs" here and there to tell you of their displeasure when you leave.

If you want an emotional supporter, then the dog is usually on a leash and attentive only to the one whom it has bonded with, while keeping pretty quiet for the majority of the time (by desire, not the dog's choice).

But if you want a guard dog, then that puppy is a little feral, sleeps outside of the home that it is protecting, and will bark at anything deemed "too close".

Every dog has its purpose for being in the home - and that purpose is defined by the owner of the house. But what happens when you want a dog who can offer comfort when you are upset but you leave them outside all of the time? Or if you want a guard dog but you buy a retriever that would be better suited to play with an intruder to death than to chase them away?

We can say we want certain things and have a purpose for them all we want but our actions and interactions will prove or disprove our words pretty quickly.

We only need to see what direction the feet are facing to know whether the end goal is a real destination or a fantasy. **We cannot wish things into existence.** No more than I could wish the Chihuahua into a silent night. Everything needs constant training, reevaluation, and guidance.

So what is the purpose of a guard dog at the Ugly House? Especially so early in the work? When we come to see the house as valuable not because of its condition but because of whose it is and the importance of the work being done, then the intention of a guard dog comes more into view. You see, we only protect what we value.

And this added layer of protection is only as good as our involvement in it. Because there are good guard dogs and there are bad ones, but the owner of the house chooses.

In Genesis 2:15 the scriptures say that God placed Adam in the garden to "work it and keep it." The word used in the original text for "keep" has an underlying layer beyond just pulling up the weeds as a form of good stewardship or gardening. To "keep" the garden, God used the word that can also be translated as "protect" (Good Boundaries and Goodbyes, Lysa Terkeurst)[10].

God didn't just want Adam to manage something that He created, He wanted Adam to actively protect God's creation as he worked on it.

Why would a garden need protection? Especially if sin had not entered the world so the infrastructure had not been broken yet?

Enter the snake. Even in the garden, a predator loomed about.

We know from the book of 1 John that Satan's intentions have always been to "steal, kill, and destroy" and the beginning was no different. God was not unaware of the snake. It didn't slip past Him. Pun intended.

God spoke to work the ground and to protect it because all of God's goodness and all of the growth were vulnerable and needed intentional guarding. It was Adam's job. It was his purpose.

When we read the story of Creation we don't know how long it took for the snake to slither into Eve's DMs to plant ideas about God's character and an alternate version of their vision of the garden, maybe they lasted a few years. Maybe a week. Maybe a few moments. But no matter how much time it took or didn't take, Adam failed to protect it because the temptation didn't come from a snake - it came from his wife. He might not have known even what to look for as he gardened and worked the land day after day, but surely it wasn't the flesh of his own flesh hand-crafted by God Himself. It was the blindside of all blindsides.

There is a lot of talk about Eve and her destroying everything. It is like a right of passage for a woman at some point in her Christian journey to mention wanting to "talk to Eve" when they get to heaven after enduring 20+ hours of labor or having an especially painful menstrual week. We give this woman a lot of flack but may I offer that scripture says that sin entered through "one man" (see Romans 5:12-19) and him being Adam.

You see, God's instructions for the garden were spoken to Adam before Eve was ever formed. She might have known God's vision of how they were to live by her husband sharing and showing her, but the Scriptures never depict the Lord speaking to Eve about it! This is pretty pivotal because if we understand that Eve took her advice from her husband, it wasn't as clear, and not just because it was coming from a man. No shade here. Truly. The point is that it was secondhand.

Eve was manipulated and fell into the temptation of chasing her desires (the whole story depicts that the food looked good and *probably* was good to eat), but Adam was the one who openly defied God and sinned.

James talks about this slippery slope of temptation. Before sin is ever a willful act of disobedience, it is first introduced as a temptation. It says: "But each person is tempted when he is lured and enticed by his own desire. Then desire when it has conceived gives birth to sin, and sin when it is fully grown brings forth death." (James 1:14-15)

We've talked about the reason Jesus had to come, and we've talked about what would have happened if God had let them stay, but can we unpack for a moment that it wasn't Eve's sin? It was Adam's. But Eve birthed into existence the seed of mistrust that would lead to our ultimate fall.

This all leads us back to the purpose of the guard dogs, protection. Adam was charged with this task and failed because he might not have imagined that it would come how it did. Satan is crafty in this way. And while we could pout that he continues to use this craftiness to upheaval our own lives, we could also learn how to fight back.

It starts with the right dog.

If you were to scour the internet for the best guard dog to protect something of great value, you would not choose my mother's Chihuahua unless your imagined predator is 12 inches tall. Nothing beyond that would be intimidated no matter how loud the bark was.

We pick our guard dog not by our connection to them, but by how we value what they protect and by how big we imagine the threat to be.

Are you valuable? Are you of worth? Do you see how conniving and manipulative and untrustworthy Satan is as he will use even God's words to temp and pull you away?

Who have you placed in your life to sound the alarm when danger is getting too close to home? Are they really up for the challenge?

Here's another question (as if I haven't asked 5 already), are you? Will you be willing to share the temptations that knock on your door in the cover of the darkness at night? Will you alert the guards when something has snuck by that is too gruesome (we believe) to uncover? Or will you trust the guards when they've made a big ruckus over something that you see as innocent?

Dogs don't always get it right. But what is the purpose of a dog if they don't know how to protect or aren't really given the permission to?

If you have ever wondered if you were worth it, you are.

If you've ever struggled with seeing a way out of the constant traps, there is one.

Ask the Lord today, who is the guard dog that you've given to me at this moment in my life? Who has been purposed to help me protect what you are working on?

And please do not tell them that I likened them to an animal. The imagery helps us see more clearly, but also yes they should have a little fight in them. When you realize that you are in the fight for your life you choose differently.

If Adam knew who was speaking to his wife, and what the ramifications would have meant, he would have acted differently.

A good guard dog is a little hard around the edges and holy.

They speak up when it is more comfortable to stay silent, they ask questions that most would rather leave unanswered. Sometimes they are sisters or brothers, mothers or fathers, but oftentimes they are also older saints in the church or coworkers from a different congregation. They see us in our floundering and fumbling, and their love is often seen as tough.

They see the value in the house and know how to remind you when you've lost your way. They don't give up or give in.

They also have to be asked. Invited into close proximity.

Dogs don't just show up in yards.

When I reflect on my journey of salvation and transformation, I can't help but be grateful to God for allowing us to be seen in this way by others. As a young youth pastor, there were many decisions made that were non-Mal-intentioned but maybe without wisdom. One such action caused a stir so large that I recieved a phone call from a pastor I served just to tell me how poorly she thought I was pastoring, using all of the harshest choice words.

I was devastated. I looked in horror into my husband's eyes as she berated me, him begging to have the phone and my utter shock that caused me to be frozen in position not letting him.

He stormed into another room and called the man who was my youth pastor as a teenager. A man of character and full of faith who had moved me into his home during Bible college because his family had a special fondness for me. I never could understand why.

As soon as my call had ended, with tears still in my eyes, my husband Rich pressed his phone to my head and said that Pastor Joe wanted to talk to me.

I imagined that after Rich shared what had happened, I would get a soft word of validation and comfort. That I would be built up and encouraged, told to not let any of the misunderstood and misguided words penetrate my heart. What I got instead was a lot like an unwanted bark.

When this woman spoke the hurtful words she did, they were not the first I had heard them. I had been saying them of myself for years. That I wasn't good enough to be in ministry. That I was ruining everything. I was about to let an old friend back into my home, but Pastor Joe could feel the presence of Failure lurking by my door to come in and take up residence, and chose to instead urge me toward forgiveness.

Seriously, at a time like this, he was asking me to forgive. Something that had only just happened. But still, here I was, phone in hand in disbelief that someone who loved me as a father would a child would not comfort me with words of validation that just argued with the words my own body wanted to agree with. He knew the only way to war off the identity-destroying thief was through a holy act of letting go.

Failure wasn't welcome in my home. Instead, Forgiveness sat with me and wiped my tears.

If Rich had not called to share everything that was happening and if Pastor Joe had not been so in tune with the heart of God, I shudder to think where I would be to this day. Surely not in ministry. Look what ministry had done to this woman. She reacted so strongly to me because she had already been unraveled by a thousand more conversations and attacks. Her enemy was great, but God is greater still.

My friend, you are worth the fight. You are worth doing the hard and holy things.

It is time to pick the right guard dogs who won't just fluff your feather pillows but will stand watch over your life to preserve what God is doing because the liar himself will come in many forms - and if we don't have the right people surrounding us **we may just befriend what God is telling us to go to battle against**.

personal reflection

1. Who is your go-to "person" or small group of people? The person you ask advice of and share details of your life not given to the general public?

2. Do those you've given unfettered access to your life have a personal relationship with the Lord? Does their wisdom reflect God's character and their instruction point you in the way that God sets out for us in scripture?

3. How might having a spiritual mentor who encourages your journey to know God more and reflect His love more in your life affect your overall health?

CHAPTER TEN

Pictures on the Wall

Should you find yourself in my mother's home, you will undoubtedly find a much younger version of myself in the frames that encompass her walls. Many much younger versions of myself. Throughout all of life's stages. She cherishes them, and after my brother passed a few years ago, I understand their priceless value and nature now, too.

I just wish they weren't, so matter of fact. A photograph is the exact thing it sees. There is no filter on those 1990's polaroids. Just pure, unadulterated childhoods unbothered by cultural acceptabilities and YouTube makeup tutorials. My children have very different, perfectly crafted pictures hanging in my own home. The two, I can attest, are not the same.

And while I still laugh at the hairstyles and more often than not, moody faces, I smile as I linger around each one. These were moments in time curated for me to cherish for the rest of time.

There is no brushing up or glossing over - they speak the truth exactly as it were.

When I think about looking upon the walls of the Ugly House, these are the kinds of images I imagine. Moments in time that explore and explain each life stage and milestone. A visual photo guidebook that narrates the backstory of who we've all become. Of course the pictures themselves only serve as a marker, you'd have to inquire to the whole story.

Which, of course, many visitors have taken up as they gleefully walk the halls of the house, pointing to each new era with the same expression a pirate might make upon discovering a new treasure. I am not as elated.

It was this comical showcase that was brought to mind recently as I attended a Minister's Retreat. The speaker, a well-spoken and educated leader for the prominent social compassion organization Convoy of Hope, was unpacking the depth of experience that Isaiah had as he poured out his vision onto the pages of scripture.

Dr. Heath Adamson drew the attention of the audience to the contents of Isaiah 6 as he read aloud: "In the year that King Uzziah died, I saw the Lord, high and exalted, seated on a throne; and the train of his robe filled the temple." (Isaiah 6:1)

What followed next was an overview of the great loss that the kingdom felt, especially Isaiah as a prophet who had the ears of kings and leaders, as King Uzziah was a man known for bringing prosperity and security to the kingdom of Judah. Unlike those who would come before or any that would come after, King Uzziah led the nation to the height of its power[11]. And when King Uzziah died, despite finishing his final days isolated and stricken with leprosy after becoming emboldened to burn incense in the temple (a task specifically noted only for the descendants of Aaron that caused God's punishment in response), the kingdom found itself in great mourning. In this state of national and personal insecurity, uncertainty, and grief - Isaiah has a vision with the Lord.

There is just something about the reminder of God's supremacy and sovereignty that allows our worries to be quieted - but this image is something so much more powerful that I knew this chapter must be added. *(You know, because I technically finished the manuscript but God nudged for me to open it back up and slip this chapter in.)*

As Dr Adamson began to explain the cultural context of what Isaiah was envisioning, my eyes began to well up with tears.

The train of a king's robe was elongated with scraps of a defeated king's robe so the longer it trailed behind him the more victories he had accrued. It was his record, his stats, his proof of greatness. Every inch was a reminder that the king had withstood the nation's foes... and won.

And the word used in Isaiah 6:1 for "filled" is a Present Continuous word in the Hebrew language which in simple terms means, it is a continually ongoing action. The Lord's robe didn't just fill the temple in which Isaiah was standing, it would always and continually fill the temple no matter how large or how expansive the room. Because **there is no end to the victories that God has won.**

He just keeps winning.

Let me circle this back for us because there is a reason that I couldn't allow this book to be complete without the image of the Lord's robe on its pages.

The pictures we plaster on social media, the awards we hang up for all to see, are all scraps that we are sewing to our own lives to prove our worthiness for others. We tote them around for accolades and accredit to ourselves some measure of triumph but they are nothing in the court compared to God.

The scriptures say, "All of us have become like one who is unclean, and all our righteous acts are like filthy rags" (Isaiah 64:6).

It doesn't say the sinful things we do, it says it is the righteous ones that are still filthy rags to God.

It is never good enough.

Please stay with me, because that is good news. It was never about our robes.

While we are posting pictures for approval and validation, God is hanging photographs in our homes. He is marking the times that we have been changed and renewed. He is keeping track of the eras that we move closer and closer to Him. He is not embarrassed by how small we began, He is intently looking over the growth of our lives with adoration as a Father looks over His child.

Your robe doesn't need to fill the temple, and neither does whomever you are putting your trust in because God's already is. His work is enough. His work is more than enough.

His work is without end or rival. He is neither threatened nor discouraged.

And while we are recounting our righteousness to justify why God should love us, God is wrapping our very beings in the same rags that His Son was buried in to hold us as tightly as we will let Him.

There is no shame in the childlike faces that fill the frames of my mother's house. I was once a child. But we were never to stay in that place.

"When I was a child, I talked like a child, I thought like a child, I reasoned like a child. When I became a man, I put the ways of childhood behind me. For now we see only a reflection as in a mirror; then we shall see face to face. Now I know in part; then I shall know fully, even as I am fully known." (1 Corinthians 13:11-12)

There is this forgotten truth that we have all not yet arrived. We are headed somewhere. Toward the likeness of God who created us in the beginning in His image.

What was broken in the garden will be restored, but it happens day by day, wrinkle by wrinkle. It is a thousand moments and a thousand days walking in the direction of the narrow way. We may not recognize the change our inner souls experience but the pictures on the wall mark the way.

We were once children, and look how we are growing.

Throughout time, there has always been a tradition to mark something or hold onto something to be able to look back and remember what has happened.

We see it in the story of Joshua crossing the Jordan River, instructing the Israelites to pick up the dry rocks from the riverbed where the Lord held back the waters to tell their future children what God had done (see Joshua 4). We see it in the tradition of the peasant shepherds who would carve symbols of God's providence and deliverance into their staffs to share with others around the fire. Something that David wrote in Psalm 23 was a comfort to him. And we see it in the train of the king's robe as he would sew his victories one after another to the end of it as a symbol of power and victory.

The pictures on the wall serve as our markers for what God has done.

They hang in our homes to remind us of all of the ways that God has come through, supported, comforted, delivered, and even healed. They are displayed for others to inquire of and peer into as we retell God's goodness over and over, knowing that we will never run out of wall space for God to continue filling our lives.

It happens one inch at a time, so it is easy to miss, but friend - don't you realize? You're still here.

Whatever you have faced, whatever you continue to face, God has awoken you to another day, and with it comes the potential for more light to break through.

Please believe me when I say, **there are frames that have yet to be hung.** God is not done with you.

When you are feeling defeated and alone, remember that it isn't your train that counts - it's His. And He has never lost.

Take a moment to wander around and gaze into the journey that the Lord has led you on. He has never left you or forsaken you. And He isn't done with your story yet. Hold fast. Hold tight. God will surely come through.

personal reflection

1. If your spiritual life were to be documented by images, what would they be?

2. How might you describe your first meeting Jesus to someone who is looking at a two-dimensional version of it?

3. In what ways might you need to remind your soul that your performance rate is not important?

4. What area of spiritual growth can you celebrate from the last 6 months?

God has not given up on you

neighbors next Door

In the beginning of this book, we met a character whose blind hope and faith made such an impression that it caused a deep curiosity to shape the daily actions of the one who would walk by. Her smile, her excitement, her words of belief in the good future that she was sure was coming, made a marked difference upon those who would hear. We would call this blind optimism, but for our neighbor next door - it was faith.

Scriptures say "Now faith is <u>confidence</u> in what we hope for and assurance about what we do not see. " (Hebrews 11:1) This can be a confusing text because there are no shortages of things that we hope for, and surely not all of them should have our full confidence to come to pass. At another point in scripture, it says "Hope deferred makes the heart sick" (Proverbs 13:12). So which is it? Is hope a measure of confident faith that we are to hold to, or is it a risky longing that makes our grief exponentially worse while we wait?

What is hope and faith?

To understand these big ideas, one has to return to the context in which they were written and, therefore the language they were originally penned down in. Which is Greek. And this might come as a shock, but I am not fluent in Greek. So naturally when digging through the scriptures I open trusted commentaries and study resources to help guide my understanding. I sincerely want to have faith in God like what is described in Hebrews but more times than not it felt more like the second verse than the first - painful not hopeful, agonizing not anticipating. Looking at the heavens and wondering when God was going to intervene because it seemed to be taking forever.

A quick Google of Hebrews 11 unpacked by one of my favorite teachers who likes to take words and break them down for a clearer understanding, sent me to an article called "Staying in a Place of Faith."[12] It felt promising.

Here is the breakdown of what Rick Renner writes about the words from their Greek origins:

Faith: *pistis* - in biblical times, this word referred to a guarantee and more specifically for believers had the intention of meaning what Rick remarks as a "divine spark" from God that would <u>enable a person to believe</u>.

Substance: *hupostasis* - this compound word can literally be translated as one who exhibits "the attitude and actions of one who has determined to stand by <u>something promised</u> and refuses to budge from it".[5]

Hoped: *elpidzo* - in contrast to the idea of wishful thinking, the word used for "hoped" is actually a <u>willful expectation</u>. This means you don't just "wish" something *would* happen, you're expecting it *to* happen! And it is written with the form of a verb that explains it to be an ongoing occurence. You just keep willfully expecting.

Evidence: *elegchos* - a legal term for being able to convince someone of something. It is not just a physical artifact but also a <u>convincing argument</u> that can persuade the unsure.

Pulling all of these words together, we can see that Hebrews 11:1 shows us a picture of a person who is so impacted by God that they are able to expect what God has promised to them with a strong conviction that it will happen.

They aren't dreaming up the way they want God to answer and then holding Him to it. They aren't trying to prove that they have a measure of faith by claiming an outlandish result and "willing it into existence". They are simply holding onto what God has already spoken with unwavering dedication to the truth that "He who promised is faithful" (Hebrews 10:23).

I love this. The idea that someone can be so convinced by the God that they have experienced that they are utterly immovable in their belief in Him and His good promises and plan.

AW Tozer writes of faith: "Imagination is not faith. The two are not only different from, but stand in sharp opposition to, each other. Imagination projects unreal images out of the mind and seeks to attach reality to them. Faith creates nothing; it simply reckons upon that which is already there."[13]

And as much as faith is not absurdity, it is also not filled with anxiety. It isn't the cowering church-attender, wringing their hands in the corner at all of the devastation in the world, overrun with their lamenting that they forget the God to whom they share their laments.

A person who is unsure of the God they claim to place their faith in is like "a wave of the sea, blown and tossed by the wind. That person should not expect to receive anything from the Lord. Such a person is double-minded and unstable in all they do." (James 1:6-8) This doesn't mean we don't wrestle, we wrestle. But the wrestling is not with God's character or His promises or His goodness or His power and authority. Of those things we can be sure.

When the world is giving cause for panic, don't look for the loudest voices proclaiming that the sky is falling. Look for those in prayer who are interceding with the One who holds the power to hold up the sky. They have learned something, know something, hold onto something, that will convince even the most worried critic of God's goodness and redemptive plan working *all* things - even this - for good. Friends, this world is never without its suffering - but **everyone needs a Norma next door.**

I would love to say that I am Norma, but oftentimes I am the one saying that situations are hopeless or scary.

And while I can be frustrated in my own self for not being able to be full of certainty that God is still working His good plans all of the time, I would rather bring that disappointment to God and accept His grace and the community that He is surrounding me with.

God's plan was always for us to live in interdependent community with one another.

"Two are better than one, because they have a good return for their labor: If either of them falls down, one can help the other up. But pity anyone who falls and has no one to help them up." (Ecclesiastes 4:9-10)

We are not always going to have great days. Some days (most days even), we will be the ones with our faces to the ground in horror at the events that are unfolding, while God, with His promises of His good and sovereign will, reminds us through His written word and the spoken word of others that He is still in control.

It is funny that the times we need to know God is in control the most is when we most often feel out of control - but that is why God gives us a community. So when we fall, when we are weak, when all is dark and gloomy, those who journey with us can remind us of the very things that we know to be truth in the light of day.

Rick Renner expounded on one more verse in his article on Hebrews 11 that casued me pause. Something I want to share here for us to hold to and remember as we continue the work with the Lord of rebuilding and being made new.

Hebrews 11:1 is often quoted alongside a verse just a few lines down that says "And without faith it is impossible to please God, because anyone who comes to him must believe that he exists and that he rewards those who earnestly seek him." (Hebrews 11:6)

If we aren't familiar with the language much we would, at first glance, see an extreme form of "wishfulness" that needed to exist for us to be approved and accepted by God. This sounds exhausting. And disingenuine. Talk about fake bricks, this is an entire fake brick house that the big bad wolf could blow over with just one life tragedy. This can't be the desire for God in us, can it?

The short answer: no.
And not just no, but it's an overwhelmingly enthusiastic NO.

God has never and will never ask for us to use faith as some sort of blind optimism that speaks positive affirmations to devastating circumstances making the sole proof of our belief in Him on how well we can ignore the negativity in our lives.

Instead, we break down a few words in verse 6 and see a different, more beautiful picture altogether:

Without: *choris* - this is a locational term, meaning on the outside or apart from. Think of it as a mother who is next to their child versus a mother who has dropped off her miracle three-year-old baby, who is the greatest gift to your life, at preschool to be without this cherished relationship until pickup. Oddly specific, sure, but you can either be "with" someone or "without" them. You cannot be both when it is based on a location.

Reward: *misthapodotes* - to reimburse or repay someone for the work they've undertaken in doing a job. Essentially, when you live your life as a believer, all that you count as a loss will be rewarded in full by a loving God who sees us and, as a Father, wants to reward His kids for their good work.

This means that faith can be found as we remain in close proximity to God, as we believe not just in His existence but in His nature of loving us in extravagant ways that make our hardships hold value and worth.

He lets nothing go to waste. Nothing is a loss with God.

And here is where we find Norma. Our little old lady, perched on her porch each morning to examine the work being done.

She isn't full of ignorance or naivety, she stands watch in close proximity to examine HOW God is bringing about His goodness and restoration. Not questioning if or when it will happen.

This is why she can smile. This is why she hasn't given up. Her question is not one of wishy-washy wishfulness but of secured curiosity in her own Builder's good plans.

When I was speaking of this to a colleague, he smirked and remarked that it was like an environmentalist (or as he described, a literal "tree-hugger") strapped to a tree.

They aren't just in theory frantically "hoping" in the more known terms that the forest will be saved, hiding behind their keyboards to share opinions and outrage. No, they are quite actively protesting the very act of cutting down a tree by standing guard to watch that it will not happen.

This is not a weak stance, this is willful decision manifested through strong conviction.

It is, what the writer of Hebrews calls, the substance.

However you imagined this next-door neighbor, frail and secondary as you might have thought her to have been, I want you to reimagine her as a source of strength in the story. For her words of faith spoken that were evidenced in her watchfulness, for her encouragement to the passer-by to stop and look at what God was doing. Norma helped call our friend home.

This is the community of believers that God intends to surround us with. They are not the builders but they are the ones who call our attentions and attitudes back to the One who is and to the work that He is doing.

They are the encouragers. The challengers. The teachers and the students. They might have suffered the feelings of feeling unwanted or unneeded but I assure you they are both. If you are feeling like the church has given up on you or overlooked you, I encourage you to try again. Ask someone to be your Norma. Give them a place to speak love and truth.

We need the neighbors.

In the first letter to the church in Thessalonica, Paul writes out some instructions for the believers as they live in community with one another. I love this passage and thought about sharing bits and pieces but honestly, all of it is good and needed as we walk out the ways of Jesus. It says:

> But since we belong to the day [*meaning to the Light as children of God*], let us be sober, <u>putting on faith and love as a breastplate, and the hope of salvation as a helmet.</u> [*Notice the high importance of faith, love, and assured hope of salvation being armor to protect the most critical parts of our lives.*] For God did not appoint us to suffer wrath but to receive salvation through our Lord Jesus Christ. He died for us so that, whether we are awake or asleep, we may live together with him. <u>Therefore encourage one another and build each other up,</u>

just as in fact you are doing. [*This is our responsibility to each other, we are needed in the work!!*] Now we ask you, brothers and sisters, to acknowledge those who work hard among you, who care for you in the Lord and who admonish you. Hold them in the highest regard in love because of their work. Live in peace with each other. And we urge you, brothers and sisters, <u>warn those who are idle and disruptive, encourage the disheartened, help the weak, be patient with everyone.</u> [*This last part is given with "urgency"... it is a vital marker of our community with one another as we live in such a way that is so connected to be affected by one another's journey.*] Make sure that nobody pays back wrong for wrong, but always strive to do what is good for each other and for everyone else. Rejoice always, pray continually, give thanks in all circumstances; for this is God's will for you in Christ Jesus. Do not quench the Spirit. Do not treat prophecies with contempt but test them all; hold on to what is good, reject every kind of evil. **May God himself, the God of peace, sanctify you through and through. May your whole spirit, soul and body be kept blameless at the coming of our Lord Jesus Christ. The one who calls you <u>is</u> faithful, and he <u>will</u> do it**. (1 Thessalonians 5:8-24)

Right now our house is situated among a line of college residents that change out every year. And while most days I love the sense of vitality that exists as I observe many taking early morning runs or waiting quite literally right outside of our door for the bus while I try to shuffle my children out the door for school, there is one thing that has always bothered me.

It isn't the late-night gatherings that keep up my children with the loud music that bleeds through the walls.

It isn't even the nude sunbathing that happens within a visual line of our kitchen sink as it is situated facing the neighbor's backyard. I do the dishes in my house so my husband and sons are spared the show.

The most difficult thing for me about living in a college town, the thing I complain to the Lord the most about, is the constant changing of my neighbors.

I long for the days where you forgot to grab eggs at the store and rush over to your long-time friend Norma's house to borrow an egg or two for the dinner that needed to be in the oven 20 minutes ago.
I can't help but think how wonderful it would be to phone a friend to ask if they still see the kids playing outside or to ask if they have time to join you at the park.

The constant changing of residents leaves one to feel alone and unknown.

Sure, being known is hard, too. I don't want to gloss over the equally hard moments - such as a neighbor waltzing into your house while you are in the shower, and opening the door to your bathroom to ask a question that could very well have been texted or asked when you were dry and mostly dressed. Yes it happened.

But the idea that you can be so connected, to feel comfortable enough to be in the presence of a person at their most vulnerable, also means that I would in turn have no hesitations when my son's defiance has gotten the better of me to phone and ask for some help. Or to waltz myself over no matter her day, to throw myself on her couch and cry a million tears when the world has become too much.

When we engage in the "too close for comfort" community we get to experience the ever-present reality of God and His people who are ready and willing to jump in.

We don't hesitate. We don't worry. We just come.

The beauty of Norma is more than just her resolute faith and words of trust in God. Norma was always right where she could be found. Norma was praying *and* present.

personal reflection

1. If you were to list out the closest friendships and connections that you have, would you say that many if not most (or all) still have some level of hesitation attached to them?

2. What would being completely vulnerable with a community of believers look like?

3. How might you put into practice the instructions that Paul gave to the church? Where might you be the neighbor and where might you be in need?

promises
TO HOLD ON TO

Therefore, brothers and sisters, since we have confidence to enter the Most Holy Place by the blood of Jesus, by a new and living way opened for us through the curtain, that is, his body, and since we have a great priest over the house of God, let us draw near to God with a sincere heart and with the full assurance that faith brings, having our hearts sprinkled to cleanse us from a guilty conscience and having our bodies washed with pure water. **Let us hold unswervingly to the hope we profess, for he who promised is faithful.** And let us consider how we may spur one another on toward love and good deeds, not giving up meeting together, as some are in the habit of doing, but encouraging one another—and all the more as you see the Day approaching.

if you...   *then God...*

are faithful with little	will make you ruler of much	MATT. 24:25-2
believe in Jesus Christ	will give you eternal life	JOHN 3:16
trust God and ask for wisdom	will give you an answer	JAMES 1:5-6
ask, seek, knock	will give, be found, open to you	MATT. 7:7
love God and follow His calling	will work everything for good	ROM. 8:28
are strengthened by Christ	nothing is impossible	PHIL. 4:13
will give your anxieties to God in prayer	will give you an unknowable peace	PHIL 4:7-8

belssed when we believe Him Blessed is she who has believed that
the Lord would fulfill his promises to her!

Blessed is... you will recieve...

Blessed is...	you will recieve...	
the one who perseveres through spiritual trial	the crown of life	JAMES 1:12
the poor in spirit	the kingdom of hevaen	MATT. 5:3
the one who mourns	comfort	MATT. 5:4
the meek	the earth as an inheritance	MATT. 5:5
the one desiring righteousness	your fill of righteousness	MATT. 5:6
the merciful	mercy	MATT. 5:7
the pure in heart	the sight of God	MATT. 5:8
the peacemakers	the name - child of God	MATT. 5:9
the persecuted because of their faith	the kingdom of heaven	MATT. 5:10

Conclusion

"And I am sure of this, that he who began a good work in you will bring it to completion at the day of Jesus Christ." (Philippians 1:6)

I have lived most of my life as a chronically exhausted perfectionist, striving for the highest mark of expectation. When the Lord saved me, the mark changed. No longer was I needing to be the best daughter or smartest student, instead I desired to be thoroughly holy.

And hey, this is a really frustrating goal.

In scripture God says to "be holy for I am holy" so I have rightfully pursued holiness but I have done it in a way just as suffocating, as if it were the gauge that would validate my salvation. Which of course leads to a lot of feelings of failure that just agree with the internal dialogue that I am already having about being a failure.

It's a vicious cycle.

I had become so consumed by my pursuit that I had no idea it was killing me. How can this be if God Himself is telling us to be holy? Could a loving God expect the impossible from us?

No. The proof of our salvation is not our perfection. When we accept that Jesus is the Way, the truth, and the life, it is often an inner work that only for some is visible right away. More often than not, it takes years of God working in our lives to find that our inner salvation has made it to our outer sensibilities. Because, like cleaning, some things take time.

The proof is not the product, what we can show, the proof is the devotion to the process. The showing up day after day and willingly "denying ourselves" *(our fleshly desires that are contrary to God's order and plan)* "and picking up our crosses to follow Him". The scriptures intentionally call this a daily action because daily we are given the option to choose the Way of life or the way that leads to death.

This process has a name. It is called sanctification. It is the very idea of what Paul describes to the Philippians when he penned: "Therefore, my beloved, as you have always obeyed, so now, not only as in my presence but much more in my absence, **work out your own salvation with fear and trembling, for it is God who works in you, both to will and to work for his good pleasure.**" (Philippians 2:12-13)

Sanctification is work. Active work. *With* God.

My husband is a CrossFit coach, which he loves to remind me means exercising for "functional fitness." If you have a loved one who uses this type of training, I imagine, as I have, that you have heard much about it. There is a real devotion to the kind of working out that is intended to benefit a person's everyday life. In this same way, when

Paul talks about working out "our own salvation" with God, who is also at work, he is showing us the image of a trainer who is active in an athlete's training. They have a goal and a method. They are working toward health and every day they show up they are one step closer.

Injuries will still come. Sickness will still come. There will never be an "end date" of arrival, but the goal is showing up and growing stronger day by day.

And when we imagine ourselves as the Dream House instead of the Ugly one, then the goal is more understandable as a house is never kept perfectly clean no matter how hard you may try. If you were to live alone and not even disturb the sheets to sleep on them, there would still be dust and cobwebs to address.

This is our goal, too. Not perfection, but showing up for the work because we trust the Trainer, the Builder, to know what we do not.

Brother Lawrence once said of sanctification:
"That our sanctification did not depend upon changing our works, but in doing that for GOD's sake, which we commonly do for our own. That it was lamentable to see how many people mistook the means for the end, addicting themselves to certain works, which they performed very imperfectly, by reason of their human or selfish regards. That the most excellent method he had found of going to GOD, was that of doing our common business without any view of pleasing men, [Gal. 1:10; Eph. 6:5-6.] and (as far as we are capable) purely for the love of GOD." (Brother Lawrence, The Practice of the Presence of God)[14]

The most difficult part for me is that **this process is as slow as our lives are long.** That we reach the goal only upon death. That there isn't truly something to be achieved but a journey to be a part of. But this lifelong pursuit of God is what it looks like to walk the Narrow Road spoken of in scripture.

God's way isn't oppression; it is freedom through submission to Him.

An upside-down way of living for sure, but should we trust Him, a life more abundant than we ever knew could exist.

When we understand that the Dream House doesn't look like the Dream, that it is just a normal home filled with love and light - being worked on and kept with intentional care - then our everyday mundane becomes the joy that we've been waiting for. We don't have to save our celebrations for when we die. Heaven isn't the carrot on the end of the stick keeping us all in line. God's vision is to bring "heaven to earth." For the holy to mix with the humble. To experience both in the imperfect *here*.

Might we have enough grace for this? Might we be able to put our ideas of holiness aside to experience the goodness of the grace of Jesus both for ourselves and for others?

Because we aren't the only Ugly House... there is a whole world that God sent His Son for - He wants to redeem all of us.

After the death of my brother in 2018 my family was left with a difficult decision. My father, sister, and I had all been planning to join a ministry team in Lebanon just one month later and on my brother's deathbed, he told us that we had to go. It felt a bit like a betrayal to fly across the world and experience anything of value so soon into our grief but the thought of disappointing my brother's wishes was even harder to bear. So we went. A welcome distraction that only God could have set up.

It wasn't until we were there that I realized just how my addiction to perfection could hinder the same ministry that God wanted to use to bring others to Himself. Because a part of my family was joining me this trip after I had already previously gone, and while that would have been a thing to celebrate it also exacerbated a lot of feelings that I had suppressed.

Like not having the approval from my father to go into ministry who understandably told me not to do bible school because there was "no money in ministry".

Even worse, my older sister had been through the same program and entered ministry but her first husband had been a very difficult person for me to respect and it caused me to withhold my own approval from any ministry that they had done together early on. Something that wasn't even all that apparent to me as she had been through the wringer with this man and then divorced him, choosing a very different path from my own. Her story would include a lot of things that I firmly believed against - because Jesus said so - and engaging in small talk felt impossible as I juggled the line between what was affirming these decisions versus what was just holding conversation. Of course, I went too far in the middle of the night while in a foreign country just 30 days after losing my brother and ended up causing my sister so much hurt that she phoned home to tell her boyfriend that she wanted to leave immediately.

I couldn't accept grace for myself, so giving it to someone else felt impossible when I didn't really think they even wanted it. I was so embarrassed (and exhausted) that I was overcome with nausea and ended up spending some time in the bathroom hugging the toilet. There's no sugar coating it, this was spiritual arrogance, and I had become the very thing I read was repulsive to the Father who loved me so dearly - a Pharisee. Wanting to know God myself, but keeping Him out of reach for anyone else.

I would love to say that the rest of the trip went well and that we were able to come together again but honestly - it took a long time.

I watched as my father celebrated and cheered, taking videos of my sister singing in the churches that we visited while not being present while I would speak. The Lord had given my sister and I very different spiritual gifts and it felt like I was a child again with the "lesser skills".

My face was so downcast that a few of the other women on the trip started making note of it. Where had the vibrant and passionate preacher gone that had come the previous trip? I wanted to shout that my brother was dead and my unsaved sister was being celebrated by my father who I felt was never proud of me. Me. The child who obeyed all of the rules. The one who never pushed back. I was compliant and excelled in school. Still, I was the girl with no one in the audience while I accepted my awards. It felt as though it was never good enough.

In the middle of my sorrow, I realized what I was becoming. My father wasn't celebrating that my sister who was living far from God was singing again, he was seeing his prodigal daughter returning home. Maybe she wasn't fully there yet but he could see her turn on the horizon and it filled his heart with hope. And there in the prodigal story, I had found my own character, the disapproving brother who had done everything right and felt overlooked, unseen.

Who was throwing a party for my goodness?

Just as soon as I thought it, I realized how deceived I had become. How my impossible standard of God's grace could only love and approve of those who were already cleaned up - and not the far off. How I was scaring away the very people He sent His Son for WHILE they were STILL SINNING (see Romans 5:8).

Come on, Vanessa. God's grace is for everyone. And our journeys of faith will look wildly different from one another because God is beyond time and space. His timeline is not our own. What He could have formed in my sister through her hard marriage and still serving in ministry was going to be nothing compared to the true gift of grace and love she found stumbling back into the church through a side door after many years of being away. He knew where He was taking her and I wanted to judge her every turn on the journey.

Sanctification is slow. It is messy. It often includes things that we would never choose and a hundred more that we do choose. It reminds us of both how far we have traveled and how far we have yet to go. Sanctification is both holding the gift of God and the grace of God in the same hand. And for all of the moments we wonder if we have messed it all up, God is there with a broom and a bucket to remind us that He has never given up. And He never will.

I apologized to my sister a hundred times over and still felt it was never enough. I might have caused her a few extra years of staying away from the church with a ten-foot pole but God's grace was enough for me too.

A righteous man falls seven times, but then he gets back up.

Every day. Again and again.

That is my prayer for you, for us. That while we partner with God in following His will for how He will build our lives - we also choose Him and His plans every day no matter how we might have made a muck of it the day before. Because His grace is sufficient. Jesus' blood was enough.

As the always enthusiastic wildcracker Peter encourages us: "Therefore, preparing your minds for action, and being sober-minded, set your hope fully on the grace that will be brought to you at the revelation of Jesus Christ. As obedient children, do not be conformed to the passions of your former ignorance, but as he who called you is holy, you also be holy in all your conduct, since it is written, 'You shall be holy, for I am holy.' And if you call on him as Father who judges impartially according to each one's deeds, conduct yourselves with fear throughout the time of your exile, knowing that you were ransomed from the futile ways inherited from your forefathers, not with perishable things such as silver or gold, but with the precious blood of Christ, like that of a lamb without blemish or spot." (1 Peter 1:13-19)

The phrase "preparing your minds for action" that he uses here in scripture is the same wording used for "girding your loins": the image of a man preparing for battle, tucking his long apparel into his belt to free his legs to run. Unhindered.

Preparing our minds for this pursuit of holiness will mean a lot of placing what we are trying to cover ourselves with into the truth that God has given us. It will mean addressing those things that we would rather not face to free God up to do whatever He wills. And while it might mean facing the hurts and pains of this life, it will also mean addressing the less-acceptable attitudes of our own hearts. The unforgiveness. The hatred. The vengeance. The comparison. The things that we have justified that God wants us to put in His hands so that we can run the race set before us.

God's grace gifted to us in His Son gives us the power through His Spirit to run - because He ran first.

When the prodigal was far off, the Father ran. And He has been running after us ever since. It is time to prepare to set our minds to action.

See the beauty of the Ugly House through the eyes of the Builder. See it and begin to forgive, heal, place boundaries, ask for help, invite God to lead, and continue your journey on the narrow path.

You are worth it, worth the work. Not to finally be acceptable, you already are through Christ, but to be holy. One moment at a time, one foot in front of the other.

You might have been the Ugly House, but you don't live there anymore. You are (being made) new.

personal reflection

1. How does internalizing the love and acceptance of God (despite our current condition) transform your ways of thinking of self?

2. How can you extend the same grace for change as a slow process to others in the faith?

Conclusion

NOTES

1. Lewis, C. S. 1898-1963. *Mere Christianity*. HarperCollins, 2009.

2. Robert Robinson, *"Come Thou Fount of Every Blessing"*, 1758

3. Tozer, A. W. 1897-1963. *The Pursuit of God*. Harrisburg, Pa., Christian Publications, 1948.

4. Lawrence, and John J. Delaney. *The Practice of the Presence of God*. Image Books/Doubleday, 1977.

5. Keller, Timothy. *Counterfeit Gods: The Empty Promises of Money, Sex, and Power, and the Only Hope That Matters*. New York, Dutton, 2009.

6. Lobo, Simon. *The Good News*, Saint Paul Street Evangelization, July 25, 2014, https://streetevangelization.com/the-good-news/

7. Lewis, C. S. 1898-1963. *Perelandra: A Novel*. 1st Scribner trade pbk. ed. New York, Scribner, 20031944.

8. Tozer, A. W. 1897-1963. *The Pursuit of God*. Harrisburg, Pa., Christian Publications, 1948.

9. TerKeurst, Lysa. *Good Boundaries and Goodbyes: Loving Others Without Losing the Best of Who You Are*. Thomas Nelson, 2022

10. TerKeurst, Lysa. *Good Boundaries and Goodbyes: Loving Others Without Losing the Best of Who You Are*. Thomas Nelson, 2022

11. Britannica, The Editors of Encyclopaedia. "Uzziah". Encyclopedia Britannica, September 28, 2011, https://www.britannica.com/biography/Uzziah

12. Renner, Rick. *Staying in a Place of Faith*, Renner Ministries, January 2, 2024, https://renner.org/article/staying-in-a-place-of-faith-2/

13. Tozer, A. W. 1897-1963. *The Pursuit of God*. Harrisburg, Pa., Christian Publications, 1948.

14. Lawrence, and John J. Delaney. *The Practice of the Presence of God*. Image Books/Doubleday, 1977.

ABOUT THE *author*

VANESSA SHEPHERD defines her most heartfelt work as sitting around tables with those in need of being deeply known. Her outrageous laugh has been dubbed the sound of "the joy of the Lord" and can often be heard amid deep conversation. Since ministry, specifically discipleship, has always been near and dear to her heart - Vanessa began early on writing her way through life, loss, and the pursuit of holiness, inviting others on the journey to deep personal growth rooted in the Word.

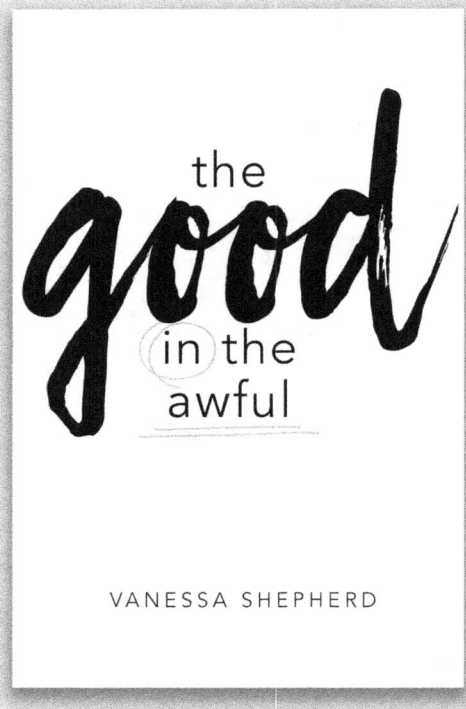

www.ingramcontent.com/pod-product-compliance
Lightning Source LLC
Chambersburg PA
CBHW050518130626
46553CB00002B/545